Crime *and*
PUNISHMENT

SHREWSBURY

Crime *and* PUNISHMENT

SHREWSBURY

MARTIN WOOD

The History Press

This book is dedicated to my wife Sue, and sons Paul and Thomas.

First published 2008

The History Press Ltd
The Mill, Brimscombe Port
Stroud, Gloucestershire, GL5 2QG
www.thehistorypress.co.uk

Reprinted 2011

British Library Cataloguing in Publication Data.
A catalogue record for this book is available from the British Library.

ISBN 978 0 7524 4546 5

Typesetting and origination by The History Press Ltd.
Printed in Great Britain

CONTENTS

FOREWORD

Martin Wood has been the town crier for Shrewsbury and Atcham for the past twenty-two years. In that capacity he has represented his town of Shrewsbury, the county town of Shropshire, and Atcham, a small village four miles away, at various European and world town crier championships and innumerable competitions up and down the country, and across it as well!

In his capacity as town crier, this hirsute gentle giant, Martin, stands at 7ft 2ins tall, and has visited America, Canada, Holland, Belgium and Germany, either working for various companies or promoting his town and county.

His enjoyment and knowledge of the history of Shrewsbury knows no bounds and he can be seen on a regular basis leading groups of schoolchildren on the 'Terrible Tudor Tour' (leaving the blood and gore in!) or taking adult visitors around his town on one of his many other tours including 'Spooky Shrewsbury', the ghost tour of Shrewsbury (now available as a book, *Haunted Shrewsbury*, published by The History Press), 'The streets and shutts of Shrewsbury' and 'A guided tour of the ten most historic buildings in Shrewsbury connected with the ale trade' – over eighteens only!

The idea for this book came after Martin had been involved in a local radio programme on BBC Radio Shropshire about crime and punishment; after the show had been aired a lady stopped Martin in Shrewsbury town centre and asked if the information he had spoken about on the radio could be found in a book as her father had been avidly listening to the radio broadcast – well it can now!

Martin is also in demand as a body 'double' for the bearded character Hagrid from the *Harry Potter* films, and has travelled across the country and abroad to Belgium as well as the county of Shropshire bringing the hairy giant to life.

Martin also gives talks to Women's Institutes and other interested groups on many local historical subjects as well as giving demonstrations on woodturning, his other main interest.

NOTE FROM THE AUTHOR

I must apologise most profusely for the lack of photographs in this book but if Mr Kodak and Mr Pentax had been born a few centuries earlier then we would have been alright

The author in his day clothes as the world's tallest town crier.

but oh no, they had to go and be born much too late! However there are many and varied works of exceptional art appertaining to the earlier chapters in this book in galleries around the country so if you have a few hours to spare on a rainy day then pop into them or try the web.

My thanks must go to the staff at the Shropshire Archives Centre based in Shrewsbury, for their help in letting their fingers do the walking for me along miles of records and for providing me with masses of information regarding executions in Shrewsbury; to Mr Morris-Eyton for permission to use the pamphlet pictures of executions in Shrewsbury; my special thanks must also go to Mr Geoffrey Abbott, retired yeoman warder of the Tower of London and recently retired macebearer to the mayor of Kendal who has supplied me with countless bits of information and dozens of photographs to peruse – thanks Geoffrey, the cheque is in the post! I must also thank Chris Holmes for providing me, via the internet, with many of the photographs that originate from the old suitcases belonging to Geoffrey Abbott, and Mr David Trumper for photographs of Shrewsbury.

Where possible I have included names and ages of all the main 'characters' in order that anyone researching their family history might possibly find a link. And if it does happen to be one of your relatives left 'blowing in the wind' then I won't tell a soul!

The various reports of the court cases and executions are not in any chronological order but in the order that I researched them. I have also included some information on other forms of executions around the world which I hope you will find interesting.

Martin Wood
Shrewsbury 2008

NOTE FROM THE AUTHOR'S WIFE:

Dear reader

Where possible Martin has researched the information himself but I apologise if there are any anomalies and ask that you put it down to his age – he's fifty!

Sue Wood
Shrewsbury 2008

BIBLIOGRAPHY

Lords of the Scaffold: A History of Execution by Geoffrey Abbott

Execution, 70 ways of Putting Someone to Death by Geoffrey Abbott

Rack, Rope and Red Hot Pincers by Geoffrey Abbott

The Shrewsbury Chronicle

The Salopian Journal

Shropshire Murders by the late Mr George Glover

Walton's Cuttings

Eddowes Journal

The Book of Shrewsbury by Mary de Saulles

Public Executions by Nigel Cawthorne

INTRODUCTION

According to the *Reader's Digest Universal Dictionary* the term 'execute' means:

1. To carry out
2. To put into effect
3. To produce a work of art
4. To subject to capital punishment

But for the meaning of the word 'execution' ,wham, we go to the top of the list:

Putting, or being put to death as a legal penalty

In today's modern lifestyle anyone who commits a crime can find themselves sentenced to a few days or months in prison or handed down a fine or, as we see so much in the newspapers these days, handed an ASBO. Imagine if you will a young lad of today breaking a window, damaging a car or committing a minor theft. His punishment would probably be one of the above penalties, but in days gone by he would have been ordered to spend time in the pillory or stocks, he might even have been birched or, if his crime had been thought really heinous he would have been hanged – that would have stopped him!

But way back in earlier times punishment could and would be so much worse. Although you can trace punishment right back to the beginning of life (remember Adam and Eve after the problems with the apple?) it was the Romans who really turned punishment into an art.

1

THE ROMAN WAY

The Romans gave the world so much – water courses, straight roads, crucifixions? As well as being very clever at inventing and designing so many things our Roman friends were also some of the most sadistic folk around it was they that developed death by crucifixion as the ultimate punishment that could be watched by hundreds if not thousands of people.

Probably the most famous case ever written, and also the best known is the story of the crucifixion of Jesus. Many books and films have been written to tell us this most famous of stories but not many depict the real suffering that would have taken place of the poor unfortunates sentenced to this form of punishment and death. Once sentence had been passed, and probably after he had spent many years in a prison, the condemned man would first be 'scourged'. This entailed the soldiers being armed with whips called *flagrums* which had long, thin strips of leather with small pieces of stone or bone tied on the end. This was then used as a lash and the pieces of bone or stone would cut into the flesh and as the leather thongs were pulled away so it would tear the skin off the man. Some of the condemned would not even survive this part of the punishment and death came upon them pretty swiftly, and mercifully, but those who did survive would then be expected to carry their cross to the place of execution, whew!

There is a lot of discussion about whether Jesus carried the entire cross (it would literally be a large tree roughly hewn and weigh around 500lb) or whether he was tied just to the cross beam. This beam in itself would weigh around 50- 60lb on its own and that would be bad enough, especially as the soldiers would continually whip you as you paraded through the streets and if you fell down then they would lay into you with their lashes until you forced yourself to get up just to temporarily halt the pain.

Again some of the lucky ones would not survive this part of the penalty and if that happened then the bodies would be pushed into a nearby watery ditch and left. But again, some men were made of stronger stuff and continued on. Once at the crucifixion site the condemned would have his wrists tied to the cross beam, and nails, about 8ins long, would be hammered through the hands or sometimes through the wrists as this would stop the hands being pulled away by the man's weight. His feet would be tied the same way and more nails hammered through his ankles. A small wooden block, called a *suppedanem*, would be placed just under his feet so that he could, at first, take some of his body weight when he was first hoisted up onto the cross and this would give him some sort of relief.

Christ on the Cross, from an old print.

Most crosses were around 8ft in height but some, probably for more 'important' or infamous men, were much higher. Jesus' cross must have been quite tall, possibly around 10-12ft in height, as in the Bible we are told that a soldier had to put a rag soaked in wine on the end of his spear so as to lift it to Jesus' lips.

This was not the end to the suffering of those men because as their arms were fixed higher and at an angle above their body it was very difficult for the poor chaps to breathe so to give them some sort of relief they would take a bit of their weight on the block and push themselves up thus relieving the pressure a bit and allowing him to take a larger breath, but this meant that he would be rubbing his scourged back on the rough timber of the upright and cause him immense pain, so he would drop down again and once more be fighting for his breath.

A physically fit young man, once he had managed to survive the scourging and the walk to the execution site and the act of nailing him to the cross, could take two or three days to die if just left but sometimes the soldiers would break the man's legs so that he couldn't take his own weight, and he would basically strangle himself with his own body acting as the weight. The records say that Jesus took just six hours to die so his legs were probably broken and of course (as it tells us in the Bible) a soldier hastened his end even more by piercing his side with a spear.

Fortunately, before most of the nailing began, the condemned man was given a drink called *galla* this was a mixture of wine and myrrh and had a narcotic effect that, hopefully, would deaden the pain for as long as possible.

So crucifixion was a normal form of punishment during the early Roman period and many different ways were devised to make these deaths more 'entertaining' to the onlookers remember, this was the DVD or television of the times so people needed some form of 'enjoyment' to while away the time, and, of course, the Romans needed a very public way of telling the locals what would happen to them if they did not toe the line.

To vary the 'sport' and make the 'entertainment' more interesting, other types of crosses were devised such as the four-man cross which resembled a very large 'X' and, as the name implies, four men could be crucified at the same time with their heads to the centre of the X, or another form resembled a football goal post where two men would be nailed up just using one arm and one leg each – now fancy that as a deterrent on a Saturday afternoon at the 'footie' match!

Crucifixion was normally reserved for the slaves and lower classes, of which there were many. If a high-ranking Roman was found guilty of a crime that he could not talk himself out of then he was allowed to have a last meal with his family before being given a phial of poison so that he could pass away without too much fuss. Who said that the rich don't have perks!

By AD 345 Rome had its first Christian emperor, Constantine, who promptly banned crucifixion, hurrah! So great and far reaching was this decision they even named a city after him. As they no longer had crucifixions to watch the locals needed something else to while away their time between meals so they brought in the new-fangled idea of an arena. Step forward Mr Kirk Douglas, sorry Spartacus!

Here was a fixture where you could actually sit out of the cold rather than standing in a howling gale and watch your favourite team, sorry, group of slaves fight to the death in various ways.

Sometimes the slaves were given old unwanted swords and daggers and expected to fight each other until the last man was standing, at other times they just used their bare hands. The problem was that as the hero of the minute was taking his ovation from the jubilant crowd he failed to hear the gladiator creep up behind him and lop his head off!

Other, more well-built specimens were paired off against the emperor's own gladiators but again it was a bit of a one-sided affair as the slave had nothing much to defend himself with but an old sword and a bit of netting whilst the gladiator was a finely honed military fighting machine with top of the range precision weapons – any bets?

Older slaves who had passed their sell by dates and who were just too frail to put up much of a fight were tied to large blocks of stone or logs by the feet, or just one foot they had to be given a chance of some sorts and suffered the greatest ignominy of all, being fed to the lions. This was originally a punishment specifically for the early Christians but thanks to Constantine and his new ideas it was developed into another of the Roman games. It certainly saved paying them a pension.

Every now and then the slaves would be placed into two teams and would act out one of the emperor's, or his special guests, famous battles but the winners still lost because, tarrah!, in comes the gladiator blokes again and polishes off the winning team as well.

Any 'loser' not pegging it out in the arena straight away and thinking that by pretending to be dead he might get away with it would be taken down to the butchers room underneath the arena and dispatched pronto before the bits that were still wholesome were fed to the lions, 'Anyone for seconds?'

2

OFF WITH HIS HEAD

Execution by decapitation or beheading has been practiced since the ancient Chinese times although our old friends the Romans also used this form of punishment but normally only for the military naughty boys. It is widely believed that our most famous of tourists to these shores of merrie olde England in 1066, William the Conqueror, introduced beheading into England, and the first man to be executed in this way was the then Earl of Northumbria, Waltheof. Although Wal was from 'up north' he decided to make a bit of a name for himself in the Norman court and to help his cause came in on Williams's side, but by 1069 he had become a little bit unhappy with the Norman type of rule and after he had been approached by some like-minded men he had joined with some northern lads in a bit of a rebellion. The rebellion failed, big time, and the only way to get back into William's good books was to agree to marry one of Williams's nieces, Judith.

Things didn't go quite right between our pair of love birds and in 1075 Waltheof was in hot water again by joining another revolt which followed the same lines as the last one, it failed, and this time there were no more tricks, or nieces, up his sleeve. So on 31 May 1076 Waltheof was taken to a place called St Giles's Hill, outside of London, intoned the *Lords Prayer*, gave his clothes to the poor and whish, off came his head.

Decapitation was mainly for the upper classes in England and from the outset originally a double-handed sword was used, which meant that the person to be executed was expected to remain perfectly still; this had its failings as sometimes the chaps would move at the wrong time and the sword would either miss completely and leave the executioner spinning on the spot or just lop off the top of the head obviously causing considerable pain. As such the sword was a cumbersome weapon and the person who wielded it was quite unused to it and so was prone to drop the thing, it was soon superseded by the axe.

This was a curved blade that was around 12–14ins in length and had a wooden shaft measuring about 3½ft long and weighing around 8lb. There are many such axes on display around the country and a few in the Tower of London. I think the actual size and weight was a matter of choice for the executioner.

One of the axes on display in the Tower of London is thought to be the one used to behead Lord Lovat in 1747, the last Englishman to be beheaded in this country. The Yeoman Wardens of the tower carry long-handled axes, sometimes mistaken for pikes, as part of their regalia but the axes were not just for show, they had a use, they were carried when the wardens escorted

Execution by the axe.

prisoners to and from their trial and if, on the way back to the prison, the axes head was held towards the prisoner, this signified to the crowds that the man had been found guilty and had been condemned to be executed.

The Tudor period in England was a particularly gruesome time because there were over 250 crimes that carried the capital sentence and executioners in that time had a field day being kept busy lopping someone's head off almost on the whim of the local head earl.

Some of the more notable persons who came adrift at the neck were two of Henry VIII's six wives – Catherine Howard and Anne Boleyn. Their crimes, unofficially so to speak, were that they failed to produce a male heir to the throne although Catherine's main advertised crime was that she committed adultery with one Thomas Culpepper, one of the king's main advisers, not something one should do when one is married to the said king!

Lady Jane Grey was also beheaded after ruling as Queen of England for just nine days. Poor lass, she was only fifteen years old and died in 1553. She was the daughter of Lady Frances Brandon and was the great-granddaughter of Henry VIII. When she was just ten years old she

Oliver led the Republic for eleven years but was made to pay for his cheek when they dug him up!

entered service in the household of Henry's last wife Katherine Parr. In 1551 Jane's father was elevated to the peerage by being made the Duke of Suffolk and he realised that King Edward VIs days were numbered by disease; he also felt that the man who held the reins of the country at this time was the young king's regent, the Protestant supporter the Duke of Northumberland and Suffolk began taking Jane to court with him. These trips to the king's court eventually led to Jane meeting and marrying the Duke of Northumberland's son, Lord Guildford Dudley.

The Duke of Northumberland had his ear to the ground and felt that things were a-changing in Britain. To begin with the duke persuaded the king to declare that Edward's half-sisters, Mary and Elizabeth, were both illegitimate and that as such when Edward passed away the crown should go to Jane who by now had become a Protestant. King Edward died on 6 July 1553 and less than a week later Jane was crowned Queen of England.

Things didn't go quiet as planned here though. To start with Mary had a massive following in this country and the Duke of Northumberland discovered, much to his amazement, that his own supporters were fading into the wallpaper and Jane's father had even managed to get his daughter to relinquish the crown. Jane, her hubby Guildford, and her dad the Duke of Suffolk were imprisoned in the Tower of London for high treason. Jane's father was pardoned but the other two were sentenced to death; however the sentence was suspended indefinitely until the Duke of Suffolk, Jane's dad, got embroiled in a failed rebellion led by Sir Thomas Wyatt which sealed her fate.

When the news of the rebellion's failure got out, things hotted up for Jane, and on 12 February 1554 she and her husband were executed at the Tower of London. Things didn't go right for her dad either because two days later he followed in his daughter's footsteps and met the executioner, and his axe as well.

Sir Thomas More had a bit of a barney with Henry VIII in 1533 and paid for it by losing his head on 6 July 1535. More became Chancellor of England after Cardinal Wolsey had died and when Henry VIII continued in his quest to marry Anne Boleyn, More refused to recognise the Act of Supremacy initiated by Henry to gain his divorce from Catherine of Aragon; something had to go, namely Thomas' head! Just before the axe fell, Sir Thomas asked the executioner if he was allowed to move his beard out of the way, 'Lest my beard hinders the axe and I would not want anything that has not committed treason be cut'.

Mary, Queen of Scots was executed on 8 February 1587 in the great hall of Fotheringhay Castle near Peterborough, Northamptonshire, but when her son became King James I he had her body moved to Westminster Abbey.

Probably one of the most well-known executions in this country occurred on 30 January 1649 when Charles I lost both his head, his crown and, just prior to that, the English Civil War! It was normal for the executions to be held early in the morning but Charles' was delayed for some time whilst a new government wrote and passed a law enabling them to do the deed; it was not until mid-afternoon when he finally arrived at the scaffold. On arrival the king, sorry, Charles, attempted to speak to the massive crowd but an order was given for the drums to beat louder to drown him out so he just had a few words with his executioner asking him to 'Strike straight and true.' He then lay his head down on the black-cladded block, thump! and the king was no more – 'Long live the republic'.

The Republic of England lasted just eleven years. When Oliver Cromwell died in 1660, the son of Charles I became Charles II and he promptly ordered all who had been involved in his father's execution to be arrested and suffer the same fate. He even ordered three of the men who had already died, including Cromwell himself, to be dug up and rehung at Tyburn for three days before having their heads nailed to London Bridge and left there to rot, urgh!

3

TYBURN

Tyburn was the central place for executions in London. Nowadays you will not find it on any A to Z map of London but you will find it under its new name, Oxford Street, and the only mark is a small plaque set into the ground on a traffic island where the trees used to stand.

The first person to be hung at Tyburn was reportedly one Mr William Fitzrobert in 1196. Fitzrobert, or 'Longbeard' as he was known, led a revolt against a tax being levied to raise money to release Richard the Lionheart from his captives in Austria. I suppose that did not go down well with Robin and his merry men!

The Tyburn area became so popular as a place for executions that between 1196 and 1783 more than 50,000 people met their end here. Like the Romans, people regarded these events as forms of entertainment and some local business men and women even erected stands and charged the good people of London and the surrounding areas a fee for a seat to view the execution in comfort. One local lady would charge 1s and throw in a snack, but that all came down around her ears along with her stand when it collapsed killing fifteen viewers, more than were killed on the scaffold that day!

At the onset of the twelfth century Tyburn Fields, as they were known, were rough ground covering more than 200 acres with the River Ti running through them. The river had a row of elms along its banks and the Normans revered the tree calling it the Tree of Justice – these trees were then used as gallows. Up until 1571 Tyburn had a single beam where the felons were executed but as business became more brisk this was replaced by a triple beam which meant that up to twenty people could be hung at a time – that's like two football teams in one go!

During King James I's reign around 120 people were hung in a single year but by the mid-1700s thirty or forty folk a day were being removed from this mortal coil.

OLD SAYINGS, PART ONE

Two of today's sayings in almost constant daily use have their origins in London executions. To 'go west' originated from the fact that when the condemned person was taken from Newgate for the journey to Tyburn, the hangman's parade turned left, or west, out of the gate. If a prisoner enquired about someone they had not seen for a while and they were told they had 'gone west' they knew that they would not see them again.

A hanging was the equivalent to *Emmerdale* or *Coronation Street*.

How the art of hanging was speeded up by this clever invention.

The second saying, 'one for the road', originated from the journey the condemned took. It was just over two miles from Newgate to Tyburn and the journey could take a couple of hours, especially as the cortege, consisting of the condemned man's cart, the hangman's cart, the cart with the coffin on and various followers all of whom would have paid to join in, was a long one. The cortege would stop at various inns on the way to give the horses a rest and the publicans would have a field day making a profit from the crowds who followed the prisoner and the hangman, by selling ale and wine probably at higher prices! As such the prisoner would be offered a free glass of wine or beer from the publican for bringing in so many customers, before moving on, and the publican would write it off as 'one for the road', knowing he had made a handsome profit.

One gentleman who wanted to get his sentence over and done with refused the free drink and asked to be allowed to continue to Tyburn. Five minutes after he had ascended the steps to the scaffold and had been hung a reprieve arrived for him – but too late! Who says drinking is bad for you it's the hanging that does it!

4

THE GUILLOTINE

Many books and films depict probably one of the most famous instruments of death, the guillotine. Named after its inventor, Dr Joseph Ignace Guillotine, it was in virtually constant use from its inception in 1792 right up into the 1930s but it was used daily during the French Revolution. In 1792 partisans stormed the Tuileries Palace and more than 25,000 people listed as enemies of the state lost their heads. The hangman in Paris at that time was a chap called Charles-Henri Sanson who followed in his family's footsteps as his father, grandfather and great-grandfather were all in the same business. Even the hangman's daughters married sons of other hangmen and in time their children became hangmen – and I wanted to be a train driver like my granddad!

In all there were seven generations of Sansons who acted as official executioners to France. At the height of his career, Charles-Henri executed 300 men and women in just three days, 1,300 in six weeks and between April 1793 and July 1795 just under 3,000 enemies of the state became enemies no more under his professional hand.

The French guillotine was not the first of its type to be used. Halifax in Yorkshire, England, became the site of the first guillotine as we know it and was in use between 1286 and 1650, some 500 years prior to the French blade; it stood at the top of the conveniently named Gibbet Street. The structure was built of a stone platform about 8ft above the ground and had two high wooden posts around 15ft high with the blade running in a groove on the inside of each post. Once the condemned person had admitted his guilt and had been sentenced – and it was important that the condemned did admit their guilt – a long rope attached to a pin that held the blade at the top of the frame was passed into the crowd and it was they that set the machine in motion! If people could not reach the rope then just holding out their hands towards it would signify that they were in favour of the execution.

If the crime was for stealing, or in connection with an animal, then the rope was tied around a beast of the same type that was whipped so that on running away it pulled the pin out and made the blade drop, democracy at work folks!

The base was still in evidence in Halifax in the mid-1800s and was tidied up and fenced off in 1857. The blade was kept for a while by a local landowner but is now on display in the Peace Hall.

The good people of Edinburgh copied the Halifax machine around 1565. Known as 'The Scottish Maiden', within a year of its building it had claimed the heads of more than 100

An early portrait of the inventor of the guillotine. It is said that Joseph's mother went into premature labour when she heard the sound of the axe fall as she was passing an execution.

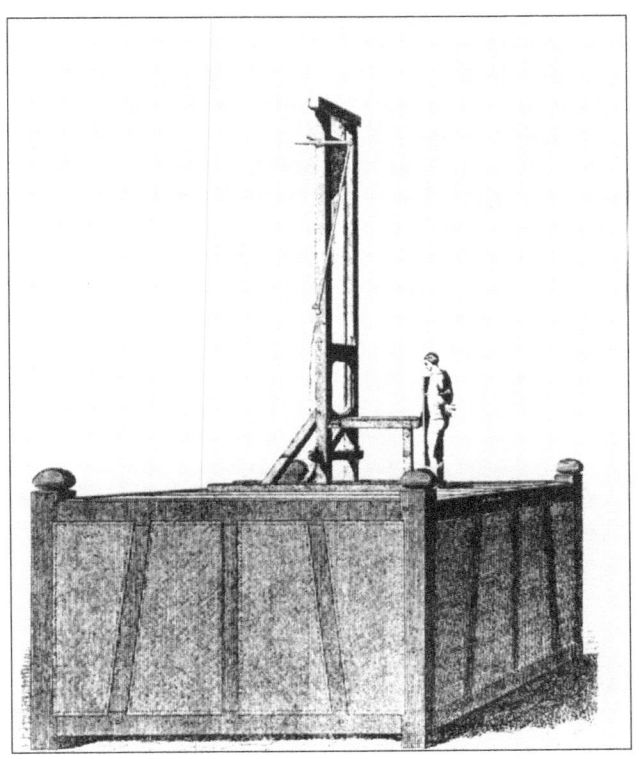

An illustration of the guillotine.

The French guillotine in action around 1857.

Democracy at work. If the crime was against a person the crowd would pull the rope; if it was to do with an animal the beast would carry out the sentence.

criminals. The only difference between the Halifax blade and the Edinburgh one was that an official executioner oversaw the Maiden's workings. It was devised by the Earl of Morton who saw the original blade in Halifax and thought it would be a good idea to have one in Scotland. He should have kept his thoughts to himself because on 2 June 1581 the earl himself was a victim of the blade.

So that gives you a general idea of the removal of felons by various means around the country so let us now focus on that wonderful gem of a town nestling in the curve of the River Severn, Shrewsbury.

5

SHREWSBURY PRISON

Shrewsbury, the county town of Shropshire, has always been the centre of trade and commerce since the Romans departed our shores and so all major punishments would have been carried out here as well. The Normans were pretty clever people because they built castles and put great big high walls around their towns that could keep armies out for great lengths of time so ... if the castles kept folk out surely they could keep folk in? Bingo! 'Let's turn the castles into prisons', which is what happened in Shrewsbury when the good old sheriff of Shropshire used the place.

In 1536 the sheriff applied to have his gaol moved from the now rather dilapidated castle ruins into the town proper, but although the move was approved nothing was done for another fifty years when reports came about that prisoners were able to unfasten their fetters and move around the gaol and even remove stones from the walls enabling them to escape into the town!

After this had occurred on numerous occasions, a move was agreed and a new gaol was built in the vicinity of what is now the town's library. Although it was known as the sheriff's gaol, and was under his jurisdiction, it was in fact owned by the Crown and by 1656 all expenses for the upkeep of the gaol were supplied by the Shropshire Quarter Sessions. Most people's idea of a gaol in this period was of a rat infested, dark, dank, windowless building, which it was, but guess what? The inmates were expected to pay rent for their rooms!

The prison then was a place of detention rather than of punishment. Whilst the men and women awaited their sentencing and wanted to make their rooms liveable, they had to work and pay for it.

In 1700, a number of the inmates imprisoned for debt applied to the Shropshire Quarter Sessions for relief as there was a danger of them 'perishing for want', probably needing basics such as food and bedding. The Sessions awarded them the sum of 1s each per week and from this time things began to change in Shrewsbury.

In 1704 the old prison was pulled down and a new one built and, for some reason, the gaoler was made to build and run an alehouse! I suppose he thought he was underpaid and needed to supplement his income, which in fact he was, and after complaining to the board of the Quarter Sessions they allowed him the alehouse and he got to keep the profits.

But still the accommodation was wanting in many ways and the new prison quickly degenerated into a 'house of vice'. In 1716 the gaoler, a widow by the name of Mrs Joan

Crumpton, complained of 'Irregularities and Misbehaviors', and even though a chaplain had been appointed in 1707 this had not helped in maintaining good order; the prisoners sent out for ale and spirits and got drunk and insulted the warders. They threw out the beds supplied and bought in their own, refusing to pay the gaol's fee for bedding! They would even have the temerity to refuse the gaoler entry into some of their own rooms, the cheeky lot.

In 1752 the then gaoler was ordered that he provided clean straw every week and obtained soap for the prisoners to wash their linen.

Alterations to the prison took place during 1776 and the chaplain, who had been appointed in 1707 on a fee of £5, had it raised to £35 per year. An apothecary was appointed in 1780 at a fee of £10 per year out of which he had to supply his own medicines. The gaolers were also given a rise in place of the profits to be had on the sale of the ale but somehow it continued to flow for many years after.

In 1793, a new and modern gaol was built on what is now Howards Bank at a cost of around £30,000. A detailed description was written at the time and this is a small extract:

> The lodges have reception cells where the prisoners are placed on entrance until they can be examined by the surgeon and cleansed. They are then sent to their proper classes and clothed in the gaol uniform, all criminal prisoners are dressed in a woollen jacket, waistcoat and cap which are coloured with blue and yellow stripes before they are found guilty but changed to brown and yellow stripes on conviction, the debtors being able to wear their own clothing.
>
> On the flat roof of the northern lodge the executions take place when all the culprits are drawn onto it to behold the mournful scene.
>
> The keeper's house faces the gate and in this is an apartment for the use of the visiting magistrate. The chapel stands in the centre of the whole and is so contrived that although everyone sees the chaplain the separate classes of inmates cannot see each other. The neatness and simplicity of its design, which is octagonal, is well adapted to the important purpose to which it is devoted.

Shrewsbury Prison was long used as a model for all new prisons in the eighteenth century and the execution stage was designed so that onlookers that stood on every vantage point around the prison saw the condemned have the hood placed over his head, but when the bolt was drawn the convict disappeared from view.

The members of the governing body that ran Shrewsbury Prison had to maintain a certain level of health and well being in the prisoners and depending on the crime or conviction they received, there was a differing level of 'dietaries', food for their comfort. For a condemned man or woman or a person sentenced to transportation or hard labour for more than three months, or for felons not on hard labour but sentenced to more than six months, they received Dietary No. 1:

- Every day each male and female prisoner to have 18oz bread
- Sunday Breakfast – 1pt cocoa
- Sunday Dinner – 1pt soup and 1lb potatoes for the males and ½lb potatoes for the females
- Monday Breakfast – 1pt gruel

- Monday Dinner – 1lb boiled potatoes and 4oz beef, cooked with no bones. Females ½lb potatoes and 4oz beef
- Tuesday Breakfast – 1pt cocoa
- Tuesday Dinner – 1pt soup; 1lb potatoes for the men; ½lb potatoes for the women
- Wednesday Breakfast – 1pt gruel and dinner the same as Monday
- Thursday – the same as Sundays and Tuesdays
- Friday – the same as Mondays and Wednesdays
- Saturday – the same as Fridays
- For supper each day – 1 pt gruel

Dietary No. 2 was for: felons who were sentenced to hard labour exceeding six weeks but less than three months; any felon sentenced to no hard labour for terms longer than three months but not more than six months; debtors were allowed a county diet (the board agreed to waive their food bills as most debtors had to pay for themselves); any man found guilty of desertion; prisoners awaiting trial or re-examination.

Dietary No. 2 consisted of:

- 24oz bread for males; 18oz bread for females each day
- Breakfasts – the same as dietary No.1 but for dinner on Sunday, Tuesday and Thursday only 1pt soup
- Monday, Wednesday, Friday and Saturday – ¾lb boiled potatoes and 3oz cooked beef with no bones
- Supper – 1pt gruel each day

Dietary No. 3 was for prisoners sentenced to hard labour for no more than six weeks and those not on hard labour for no more than three months and consisted of:

- 24oz bread for males; 16oz bread for females daily
- Sunday breakfast – 1pt cocoa
- Sunday Dinner – 1pt soup
- Monday Breakfast –1pt gruel
- Monday Dinner – ½lb potatoes and 3oz cooked beef
- Tuesday Breakfast – 1pt cocoa
- Tuesday Dinner – 1lb potatoes
- Wednesday Breakfast – 1pt gruel
- Wednesday Dinner – 1lb potatoes
- Thursday Breakfast –1pt cocoa
- Thursday Dinner – 1pt soup
- Friday Breakfast – 1pt gruel
- Friday Dinner – ½lb potatoes; 3oz cooked beef
- Saturday Breakfast – 1pt gruel
- Saturday Dinner –1lb potatoes

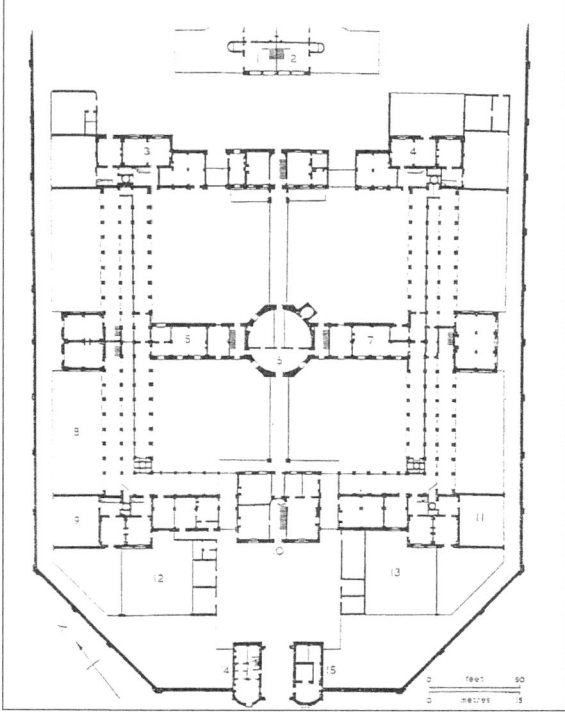

A line drawing of the ground floor of Shrewsbury Prison as it stood around 1797.

Dietary No. 4 was for prisoners who were confined to the county gaol for a term not exceeding fourteen days:

- Both male and female prisoners daily 24oz bread daily
- Sundays, Tuesdays and Thursdays – breakfast 1pt cocoa
- Mondays, Wednesdays, Fridays and Saturdays – breakfast 1pt gruel
- Supper – 1pt gruel

... You shall be taken to a place of execution where you shall be hung by the neck until dead, and may God have mercy on your soul ...

With these words many a man, and woman, and child have been sent to the gallows in Shrewsbury over the centuries, some with an air of acceptance but most still proclaiming their innocence until the bolt was drawn.

Prior to the prison being built any person found guilty of a crime and sentenced to be hung would be taken to the place where he or she had committed the crime and was executed there, although records show us that between 1787 and 1793 twenty-six people were executed on gallows set up in Old Heath. There is a little thought about what the gallows actually consisted of and how the execution took place. It is thought that the gallows at Old Heath was just a large tree and the condemned were brought to the tree on the back of a cart and once the noose had been placed around the neck the cart was moved away and the execution was over.

Other ideas were that once the prisoner arrived at the tree they were made to climb a ladder and after the noose had been fixed in place they were 'turned off', either pushed off the ladder or the ladder was twisted causing them to fall.

In newspapers of the day the reports mention that many thousands of people turned up to witness these events. As they did not have television or radio then I suppose that these hangings were the local population's idea of *Emmerdale* or *Coronation Street*.

Condemned who were executed on the gallows at the Old Heath.

(i) NAME	(ii) AGE	(iii) CRIME	(iv) EXECUTED
Richard Hail	27	Highway Robbery	31 March 1787
James Turner	25	House Breaking	31 March 1787
Charles Higley	32	Horse Stealing	27 March 1788
Richard Baydore	21	House Breaking	29 March 1788
John Pyheroe	36	Murdering wife	9 August 1788
William Bullock	19	Burglary	Defaced
Henry Morris	26	Sheep Stealing	18 August 1788
David Ellis	60	Horse Stealing	18 August 1788
William Jones	24	Highway Robbery	22 August 1789
John Jones	27	Highway Robbery	22 August 1789
Richard Price	17	Rape	22 August 1789
Thomas Phillips (senior)	47	Forgery	5 September 1789
Thomas Phillips (junior)	17	Forgery	5 September 1789
William Bonython	23	House Breaking	27 March 1790
Richard Griffiths	21	House Breaking	27 March 1790
The next seven names have been defaced			
John Mumfords	18	Burglary	10 August 1793
William Richards	18	Burglary	10 August 1793
Samuel Shelton	29	Burglary	10 August 1793
Richard Firms ton	19	Burglary	10 August 1793

In the 1700s life was cheap and an execution was so normal that the newspapers of the day just announced the trial and execution in the small print on page four of the local newspaper. *The Shrewsbury Chronicle* issued on Saturday 24 March 1787 printed the following report of the Shrewsbury Assizes held the previous day:

Death sentences were passed on the following:

Henry Foulk for being at large whilst under sentence of transportation.
Isaac Pedley for theft of six guineas out of a shop drawer owned by Mrs. Higgins and Mrs. Masefield, mercers of Newport.
Thomas Holland for robbing John Alford on the Kings Highway of eight shillings in silver, one penny in copper, a pocket book and other items.
George Vernon for stealing a sheep, the property of Mr George Forester Esq. of Willey.
Thomas Roberts alias Webster alias David Rogers for stealing a black gelding property of Mr Thomas Evans of Llanfair Caerinion.
Richard Hall for assaulting and robbing Peter Wilbraham of one and a half guinea in gold and ten shillings in silver on the Kings road in the parish of Donnington.
James Turner for burglary at the house of the Rev. Mr Rogers at Shifnal.

The judge reprieved the first six defendants but Hall and Turner lost their plea and are to be executed.

One week later *The Shrewsbury Chronicle* printed the following report:

April 7th 1787.
On Saturday last Turner and Hall were executed at the Old Heath. Their behaviour from the time they were sentenced to the moment of their departure was notable.

Hall made no confession, nor did Turner but acknowledging the justice of his sentence, and giving a short exhortation for all young persons to take warning by his fate, seemed to die in charity with all men.

That statement was printed between a report which stated that the prices of corn were 6s 3d for wheat and 3s 4d for barley and that Dr Smallbrook, Chancellor of the Diocese of Lichfield and Coventry, intended to hold a probate court in Newport the following week. See? Life was cheaper than corn!

6

TRANSPORTATION

A lesser sentence, that of transportation, was also mentioned in *The Shrewsbury Chronicle* around this time. Normally sentence of transportation would be for seven years but sometimes sentence could be for life and the recipients of this fantastic holiday offer would be taken to Woolwich, London, and loaded onto hulks. These were old sailing ships of the line, warships or East Indiamen that had passed their sell by date to await the tide before sailing to New South Wales and the infamous Botany Bay. If the ship sank on the way … well, so be it. But let's read some more of *The Shrewsbury Chronicle* reports of the Shropshire Assizes beginning with a list of names of people sentenced to transportation from the Assizes of 23 March 1787:

> The Judge ordered that the following to be transported to Botany Bay for a term of seven years:
>
> John Ingram and Edward Roberts for Perjury.
> Robert Done for stealing two and a half guineas.
> Edward Dod pickpocket.
> Robert Brown for stealing a measure of nails.
> John Brown for stealing wearing apparel.
>
> Shropshire Assizes, 20th April, 1787:
>
> 13 convicts set off for Woolwich to be placed in hulks and sent to Botany Bay.
> Last Friday was committed to gaol Samuel Pigg for the killing of William Felton of Shifnal.

Amazingly, Felton himself had been tried for the murder of a child in August 1784 but had been reprieved due to some of the evidence going AWOL. Pigg was bailed to appear in court but his trial and sentence went unreported in the paper. He was certainly never executed around Shrewsbury. Justice done?

The Shrewsbury Chronicle again:

Shropshire Assizes 22nd March 1788.

Ten people were capitally convicted:

Robert Hughes for stealing a black gelding property of Mr Joseph Barnes.

Richard Marsh for house burglary of Mr John Roden of Stanton in the parish of Shifnal.

John Hughes for house breaking of Mr Edward Jones of Squennant, Montogmeryshire, and stealing two coats and other apparel.

Thomas Weaver for stealing a white brinded cow, property of Mr Andrew Rea of Dawley Parva.

Richard Boyden for house burglary of Mr John Lea of Great Soudley.

Francis Price for stealing a black mare property of Mr Richard Edwards of Brincalett in the parish of Clun.

Mansell Powell for stealing a silver watch from the property of Mr William Duce of the parish of Clee St. Margaret.

James Dorcham for house burglary of Mr William Lowe from the parish of Tong.

Charles Higley for stealing a black gelding property of Mr Ellis Jones of the parish of Oswestry.

Richard Oakley for stealing a bay gelding with bridle and saddle property of Mr Andrew Pugh.

Seven of the above were reprieved but Robert Hughes, Richard Boyden and Charles Higley were left to be executed at Old Heath.

The Shrewsbury Chronicle announced on Saturday 5 April 1788:

On Saturday last were executed at Old Heath Charles Higley and Richard Boyden. Robert Hughes, who was expected to suffer with them, received a respite the night preceding until his Majesty's pleasure be known.

Transportation:

Samuel Pigeon was ordered for transportation for seven years for house breaking.

The noted informer Thomas Deakin was tried for defrauding Elizabeth Mathews of Fitz five pounds and was sentenced to a term of one year in prison and fined five pounds and to remain in gaol until the fine was paid.

Deakin was also tried under a penal statute for compounding a previous indictment. He was ordered to stand for two hours in the pillory in the Square on Saturday 11th April 1788 and to pay a fine of ten pounds after which he will be unable to stand as an informer.

The Shrewsbury Chronicle that was issued the following week on 12 April announced that a great number of constables were sworn in to stand guard over Deakin when he was pilloried. It is not known whether these special constables were needed because Deakin was a popular chap or because they were expecting trouble.

Executions continued at the Old Heath site until 1793. By that time a brand new prison had been built in Shrewsbury, on what is now known as Howards Bank, and that had a specific drop designed and built so that although executions could be held in full view of the spectators; as the bolt was pulled the prisoner dropped out of sight of the crowd.

Don't forget hangings in those days were not the quick clean jerks that they had in later years these were really just slow strangulations and sometimes death would be up to ten or even fifteen minutes after the prisoner had been turned off the cart.

So the last executions to occur at Old Heath took place in August of 1793 and involved four young men all in their early twenties.

The report was still on page four of *The Shrewsbury Chronicle* but they must have had a new reporter because he wrote quite an account of the actual hanging. *The Shrewsbury Chronicle*, Friday 16 August 1793:

> On Saturday last John Mumford, Richard Simister, William Richards and Daniel Sheldon alias Whiley were executed at Old Heath near this town for burglary in the shop of Mr John Jackson, mercer, of Halesowen.
>
> The unfortunate youths behaved with becoming decency and were not taken from the gaol till nearly four o'clock in the afternoon. A greater number of people assembled to see them go out than on any similar occasion for many years past.
>
> The scene was truly awful, four genteel likely young men in the bloom of their youth pinioned in a cart drew sighs and rolling tears from the multitude.
>
> The convicts acknowledged the justness of their sentence and Simister confessed to robbery of a milliners shop in Lancaster Street, Birmingham last winter belonging to Miss Waidsoe and Miss Perry and various other robberies.
>
> At the place of execution they exhorted the people to take warning by their fate and between five and six o'clock they were launched into eternity amid the cries of many spectators.
>
> Their remains were interred in a plot of ground appropriated for this purpose behind the new gaol.

So the history of the Old Heath site came to its end with the deaths of these young lads and the new execution site was awaiting its first customer, and it wasn't long in coming.

7

THE NEW DROP

A t the Assizes of 7 August 1795 reported by *The Shrewsbury Chronicle*:

John Smith alias John Urquhart received a capital sentence for a crime on the shop of Messrs. Minor and Corser of Whitchurch.

Thomas Copper for a felony and burglary in the house of Mr Nickson of Wellington.
John Jones for stealing a horse and cart property of Mr Gough of Ford.

Thomas Copper and John Jones received a reprieve but Smith was left to hang. The reporter from 1793 must have still been with *The Shrewsbury Chronicle* because a report appeared in the paper on 21 August 1795:

On Saturday last was executed at the new drop in our county gaol John Urquhart alias John Smith for shop lifting as lately mentioned in our paper.
From the time of his condemnation he discovered every mark of a true penitent and died as he expressed himself: 'A hope beyond the grave', He was a young man of strong natural parts improved by a good education but his bad company proved his ruin.

One more final report from *The Shrewsbury Chronicle* dated 18 March 1796:

At our assizes which ended on Wednesday last the five following were capitally convicted and received sentence of death:

John Hill for breaking out of gaol and appearing at large, he being under sentence of transportation.
Edward Quilt for stealing a woollen purse containing money to the value of £2 14s 8d, the property of Mr Thomas Reynolds.
Edward Moreton for stealing a piece of Irish cloth from the shop of Mr Samuel Harding of Ludlow.
Joseph Prigg and Margaret Palmer for stealing one whether sheep from the land of Mr George

Evans of Much Wenlock.

The latter three are reprieved but John Hill and Edward Quilt are left for execution.

Thomas Copper for breaking out of gaol, he being under sentence of death, but being reprieved by His Majesty's justices of gaol. Delivery was returned to his former sentence, transportation for life.

Edward Quilt was executed at Shrewsbury Prison on the morning of Saturday 26 March 1796.

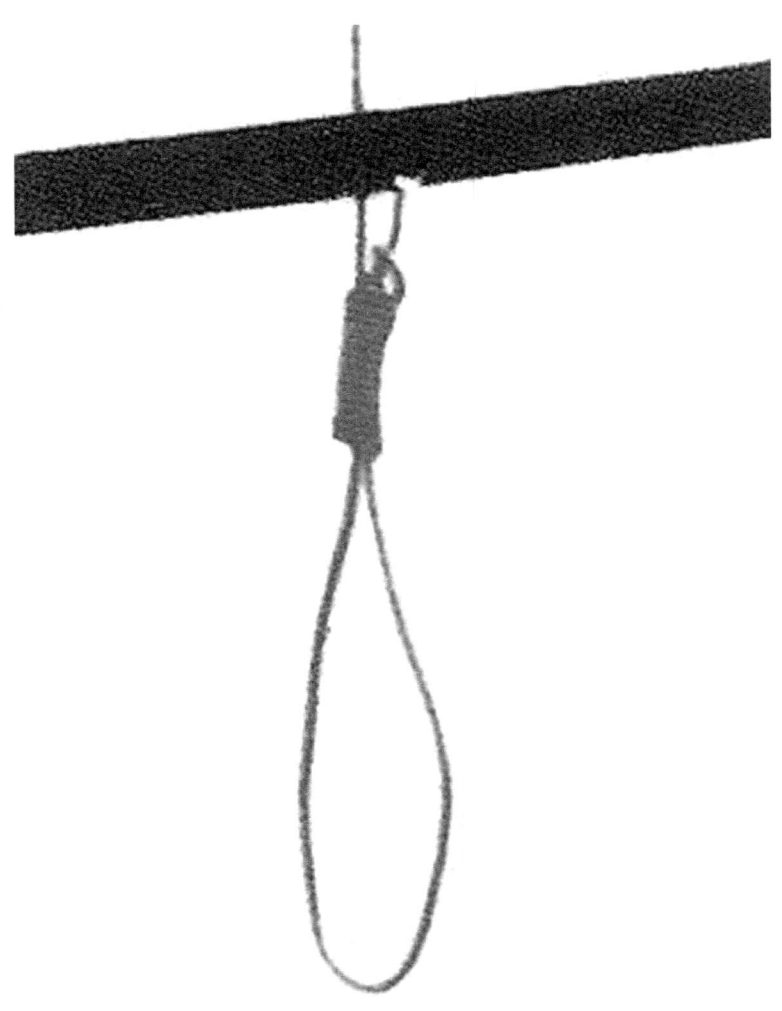

8

LONG-GONE PUNISHMENTS

Before we delve more fully into the executions of Shrewsbury let's have a look at some of the other forms of punishment that the ordinary man in the street could come across whilst waiting for his wife to finish her shopping ...

THE PILLORY

One of the most simple of designs, the pillory was normally an upright fixture of two parallel posts with a beam across the top. This beam or plank was cut in half lengthwise and had three holes cut in it: one that took the head and two for each of the arms. The recipient stood and placed arms and head in the holes and the top part of the beam was lowered and hey presto, the chap was held fast and had to take what was coming to him. The pillory stood in the market square and was one of the most popular forms of punishment in the country; it was also known as the stretchneck as this was the one part of the body that was most affected by the post.

The reason it was placed in the square was due to the fact that most of the major trading went on in the area surrounding the market hall and so it was a natural place for having as many people as possible observe the punishment being carried out. Those looking on were also able to vent their anger by throwing whatever came readily to hand, fruit, stones, animal dung, in fact the more disgusting the missile the better. Many times the criminal has died at the hands of the rabble, sometimes hired for just such an event.

Here is an early reference to the pillory:

> In 1403 Hotspur's body was removed from the battlefield outside Shrewsbury as ordered by Henry IV and be placed between two millstones in front of the pillory in the market square ...

There is also reference to the fact that a pillory at this time stood at the top of Pride Hill and Hotspur's body could have been displayed there.

In the reign of Henry VIII the accounts of the town bailiffs showed that a charge of one penny each was made against eleven men: 'for the purchase of paper to be hung around their necks by the command of the King.' The paper was used to have their crime and punishment written on them for all to see.

Also in the accounts was a cost incurred between 1519 and 1520 for the correction of a thief:

Robert Wright was a servant to Thomas Leech, a highly popular businessman in Shrewsbury.

Wright was found guilty of stealing three silver pennies from the gown of the Virgin Mary in St Chad's and was punished by being set into the pillory and then run out of town.

Wright was pretty lucky because if he had stolen six silver pennies, he would have been hung!

In March 1580 a local woman by the name of Mother Gawe was found guilty of witchcraft and placed in the pillory. Sadly no other records are available that relate to how long she was to stay there.

On 20 April 1583, James Lloyd, a servant of Sir Henry Sidney, Lord President of Wales and the Marches, was found guilty of forging his master's handwriting. He was placed in the pillory with his one ear nailed to the post and was also flogged, now that would have been painful!

In 1588 Richard Reynolds of Bagley near Cockshutt in the north of the county was pilloried for setting fire to his brother-in-law's sheep fold, killing a number of sheep in the process. This was such a despicable crime that Richard had his two ears cut off by the local executioner.

On 28 November 1613 the town hall in Shrewsbury was broken into and the sum of £29 7s 6d was stolen. Two men were arrested shortly after the crime had been committed and one, no name, was hung – yes, actually hung on the pillory until dead for his crime whilst the other was granted a free pardon as he was one of the king's millers – a case of not what you know but who.

On 12 April 1600 a servant was fixed into the pillory with a note around his neck advertising that he had been found guilty of the attempted murder of his employer, Thomas Onslow, who resided in Boreatton near Baschurch, north of Shrewsbury.

The hapless servant had applied for a wage rise and when Squire Onslow refused, the servant took his revenge by striking him with a knife taken from the dining room. It seems that Thomas was a fairly rotund gentleman who enjoyed his food, and his girth saved him because the knife could not reach any vital organs!

In 1795 a lady locally known as 'Mistress Cakes' but whose real name was Mary Evans was ordered to spend three weeks in prison for keeping an 'unruly and disorderly house' (pub). Such was the crime that Mary was also ordered to spend one hour a week in the pillory.

The local Shrewsbury newspaper reported that on 13 September 1803 a local publican was accused of short measuring – off with his head? The judges at the time though were a bit more lenient and, as this was his second offence, fined him 13s and sixpence and warned him that if he reoffended a third time then his punishment would have been a fine of 20s and time in the pillory. Whether it was the fact that he had already been fined such a large amount and could not face a higher one or that he couldn't face the pillory it seems that our publican turned over a new leaf and sinned no more, Cheers!

If these two are married then I don't give him much chance when they are let out!

OLD SAYINGS, PART TWO

Ever come across the old saying 'from pillar to post'? The old adage has its beginnings with the pillory. From 'pillar to post' now means going from one place to another without really getting anywhere fast but originally it meant being moved from the pillory to the whipping post for further punishment, so next time you are in a rut and getting nowhere spare a thought for the poor unfortunates who gave us the saying.

THE DUCKING STOOL

Originally this form of punishment was also known as the gumbolstol and was used mainly against four types of person in Shrewsbury.

Butchers were sometimes in for a ducking for selling stale or 'unwanted meat due to its odor'. These butchers would hold their markets in the aptly named Butchers Row, a short road leading from halfway up Pride Hill to the top of Fish Street. As many as forty or fifty butchers would be selling their wares and so it was quite common for some to try and make a bit on the side by cheating their customers.

Bakers would sometimes 'rise' to the bait of making a little extra dough by selling underweight bread. The weight was decided on by the town's fathers and could change from day to day depending on the price of flour so the bakers were dependent on the town crier to announce the prices at the start of each day's trading. So that the bakers could stay within the law they would sometimes put a small cob loaf in with the order, hence the term 'Bakers Dozen' being thirteen in number so as to provide customers with an order slightly over what they asked for.

Wine, or beer sellers, was the third group that could find themselves in deep water for selling stale wine and beer. Shrewsbury had an amazing amount of ale houses; Mardol had twenty-seven in a row! Beer did not keep as well as it does today but as the price of a barrel was sometimes quite high it is no wonder that some of the more, shall we say 'tight fisted landlords' attempted to pass some of the out of date or stale liquid on to already inebriated customers.

But the most common use of the ducking stool was for the punishment of nagging or scolding wives, 'Bring back the good old days!'

The siting of the ducking stool was originally over the 'Bishops Pond' in the square sometimes known as 'Bishop David's Pond', so named after the third Bishop of Wales. He supposedly visited Shrewsbury, got slightly inebriated over a few glasses of communion wine, and then fell into the pond and drowned – to make it legal they named the pond after him!

High Street was at one time known as Gumbolstrasse or 'The Street of the Gumbol Stool'. It appears that there was possibly more than one site for the stool in Shrewsbury. Lord Burleigh's map of the town shows a possible site at the bottom of the Wyle Cop near the Stone or English Bridge; another is shown near to Dogpole and another site has been mentioned near to the Welsh Bridge. One more site is thought to have been in the Quarry Dingle; certainly burnings and other punishments have been held there so why not a ducking or two as well?

The punishment for the butcher, wine merchant and baker was quickly found to be too much of an embarrassment to the men and was rapidly removed, leaving the way clear for the stool to be regarded as for women only. It has been described as being made of two parallel wooden beams about 15ft long, with a chair fixed at one end so hinged that it swung freely, keeping level whichever angle the beams were. The lady to be ducked had her hands and feet tied to the chair; once in position her weight would pull the chair under the water. She was then reliant on the Gumbol Man pulling down on the other end and so lifting her out of the water before she was once again lowered in. It has been 'suggested' that at times the Gumbol Man was offered to partake of wine or beer by the husband during the course of the punishment and so the nagging stopped for all time.

The last recorded ducking took place just over the Shropshire border in Leominster when a lady by the name of Jane Corran, also known as Jenny Pipes, was introduced to the stool which was 26ft long. Far from teaching her a lesson it appears that her first words on being pulled out of the River Lugg at Kenwater Bridge were extremely rude and aimed at the magistrates that put her there in the first place! Sadly history does not record what happened to her but I think she went back in again.

The same stool was brought out again in 1817 for the punishment of one Sarah Leeke but as the water in the river had dried up the punishment could not take place. As all these punishments attracted hordes of people there were still plenty more who could not attend and so many songs, most of them fairly rude, were penned to entertain them and pub guests around the country.

Not all ducking stools were built and used in the public gaze. The great prison reformer, John Howard, whose bust stands above Shrewsbury Prison's main entrance, wrote of a visit he made to Bridewell in Liverpool in 1779:

The river in Shrewsbury was used for ducking as well. (Picture courtesy of Bill Champion)

In the courtyard is a pump to which the women prisoners are tied every week and receive discipline. There is a bath with a standard for a long pole on one end to which is fastened a stool. In this all the females, not the males, were placed and underwent a thorough ducking repeated thrice.

I leave this part of the book in the capable hands of the composer Benjamin West who, in 1780, brought us the best, and cleanest, piece of poetry that explains the use of the ducking stool:

> There stands, my friends, in yonder pool,
> An engine called the ducking stool,
> By legal power commanded down,
> The joy and terror of the town.
>
> If jarring females kindle strife,
> Give language foul or lug the coif,
> If noisy dames should once begin,
> To drive the house with horrid din,
> Away, you cry, you'll grace the stool,
> We'll teach you how your tongue to rule.
>
> The fair offender fills the seat,
> In sullen pomp, profoundly great,
> Down in the deep the stool descends,
> But here at first we miss our ends.
>
> She mounts again, and rages more
> Than ever vixen did before,
> So throwing water on the fire,
> Will but make it burn the higher.
>
> If so, my friend, pray let her take,
> A second turn into the lake,
> And, rather than your patience lose,
> Thrice, and again repeat the dose,
> No brawling wives, no furious wenches,
> No fire so hot but water quenches.

THE BRANK

Sometimes known as the scold's, or gossip's bridle, this was a metal face mask that resembled a cage or a modern-day type of helmet similar to the ones ice hockey players wear and was just slightly larger than the lady's face. It had a tongue depressor fitted that made it nigh on

The town crier was used to advertise the lady's misdemeanours.

impossible to speak and almost impossible to swallow; sometimes the depressor would be replaced with a knife or blade that had a sharp point and was used for scolds and nagging wives after the ducking stool had been abolished in the seventeenth century.

The method of fitting the brank was easy to carry out – the back of the cage was opened (some had the opening at the front) and the lady's head was pushed inside. A rope was then passed through hoops or rings on the lower rim on back and front and when the cage door was shut the rope was pulled tight, so fixing the cage firmly in place. The scold was then either fixed to the pillory with a note pinned to her front or led through the town by the town crier who could advertise her crime and punishment.

The brank was not only used for the punishment described above but could also be found in some of the workhouses, especially in the north of the county. It was abandoned in 1825.

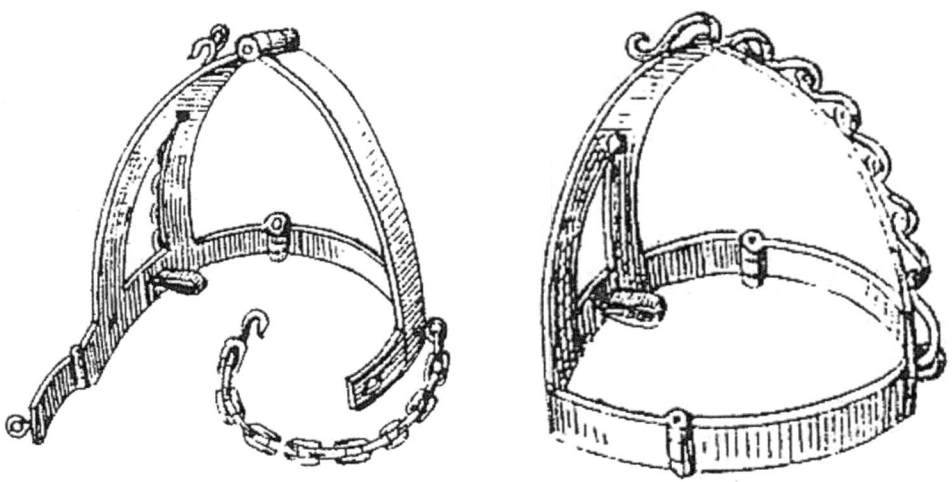

The Shrewsbury brank in open (left) and closed (right) position.

THE WHIPPING POST

Since Noah was a lad whipping has been a common punishment in all its forms – known in the past as scourging (remember crucifixions?), flogging, and flagellation. In Shrewsbury the culprit would have been tied to the pillory and a policeman, or more often the hangman, would have carried out the punishment. Sometimes the criminal would be tied to the tail of an animal and as the beast was led around the town the poor chap would be whipped on the move. At various times the punishment would call for the criminal to be 'carted' – instead of being tied to the beast he would be tied to the rear of a cart with his back bared and the hangman would stand in the cart and whip the chap over his shoulders. As the hangman or executioner was much higher than the criminal a heavier lashing could be meted out. Sometimes the criminal would be tied, spread-eagled to a cart's wheel, and the cart was pulled from the police station, where the music hall now stands in the square, to the market hall. With the whipping again continuing on the move, such was the ferocity of this carting punishment that some receivers of the whip never finished the course. A whipping post was also erected outside the old guildhall but the post hole has been lost, thanks to modern building techniques.

The records of the Borough of Shrewsbury show various entries where payment for floggings was paid:

> On January 15th 1785, Robert Cole was found guilty of wandering the Parish of Wellington begging and was sentenced to be publicly whipped from the carts tail from the Market Hall to the prison, imprisoned for six months, and then whipped again at the end of his sentence.

Another to fall foul of the whip, pardon the pun, Thomas Hughes was whipped for stealing a turkey belonging to Rowland Wingfield.

It is believed that public whipping in Shrewsbury came to an end around 1840.

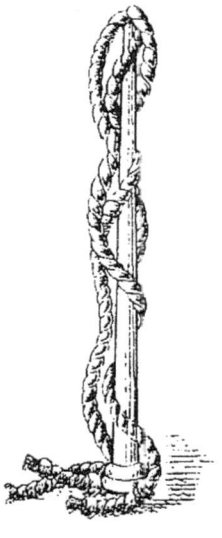

Shrewsbury whipping post.

The stocks in Shrewsbury have long gone – these were loaned to me by my friend in Kendal.

THE STOCKS

Contrary to popular belief, the stocks were not normally used as a form of punishment, but instead they were used to hold criminals under the protection of a constable until such times as the local sheriff or court could try them. It was commonplace for the victims of the crime to persuade friends to visit the thief in the stocks and meet out some form of gentle punishment. Usually, because of the proximity to the market hall and the 'green market', vegetables were used. But other more ungentlemanly missiles were sometimes used to find their mark!

The stocks were last used in 1850 when a local police constable was found guilty of being drunk. Such was the popularity of the constable that a large crowd formed and the stocks, with the constable still in them, was paraded around the town on the back of a cart and then back to the square where a local man removed his hat and made a collection for the unfortunate bobby whilst songs were sung, and his health toasted. Then the officer went home much richer than when he started out that day!

OLD SAYINGS, PART THREE

The stocks gives us another of our daily sayings: 'A laughing stock' or 'To make a laughing stock.' When the recipient of the punishment was put into the stocks they became a figure of ridicule and so was made a laughing stock; clever stuff this English language …

PRESSING TO DEATH

Between the times of Edward III and Henry IV this punishment became commonplace.

Known as '*peine forte et dure*' meaning 'severe and hard punishment', this was punishment for anyone who was put on trial for treason, felony or capital crime but refused to plead. It was paramount that the guilty party admitted their crimes otherwise judgment could not be passed but if the felon refused to plead then the jury had to decide whether this was due to '*mute of malice*' 'deliberate silence', or 'mute by visitation of God', unable to speak due to a disablement.

If the court decided that silence was down to mute of malice then they had to come up with some way of persuading the felon to talk so judgment was then given that:

> The prisoner shall be remanded to the prison and laid there in a low dark house, or cell, where he, (or she), shall be naked and that he shall be on his back and arms and legs be tied to each quarter of the room. There shall be placed on him iron and stone as much as he can bear and more and the next day he shall have 3 morsels of barley bread without water, the second day he shall have 3 drinks of water from a pond, not fresh running water, and this shall be his diet until he is dead.

Death in three ways would be involved in this barbaric practice:

1. Death by Famine
Bread alone is not good for you and the barley bread, when mixed with the brackish water would swell.

2. Death by Weight
As the stomach swells when the bread and water mixes, the added weights piled on top of the recipient would lay heavy and stop the stomach swelling until the skin burst and the contents spilled out.

3. Death by Cold
Obviously, if the poor chap is spread-eagled naked on a cold floor he could catch his death; it would save a lot of bother and pain.

Sometimes a sharp stone would be placed under the villain's back against his spine and as the weight of the stones pushed down so it would break the spine and induce paralysis, and death.

In 1771 a highwayman, Thomas Spiggott, refused to plead and was taken to the cells in Newgate Prison and had 350lb on him for half an hour. When he still refused to plead the warders added another 50lb weight and with blood streaming from his nose and mouth he eventually pleaded guilty. On 8 February 1771 Thomas was taken to Tyburn and hanged.

Some held out for longer with even heavier weights. One man called Frasier, accused of murder in 1726. held on for two hours with 400lb on him before he pleaded not guilty but they still hanged him.

It was such a barbaric form of punishment that the judge would warn the possible offender three times of the penalty if he, or she, refused to plead and they would be given some hours to respond. If they still persisted in keeping mum then judgment was pronounced on man or woman.

In the records of St Mary's in Shrewsbury a man was recorded as being buried after being pressed in the castle on 28 August 1628.

In 1772 the law began to change and from that time any criminal who refused to give a plea was deemed to be 'guilty' and hanged. In 1827 the law changed again to show that a refusal to plead could be considered as 'not guilty'.

Torture under pressure.

BURNING TO DEATH

This was the main sentence for any woman found guilty of treason from the earliest records. Burning was carried out by tying the condemned person to an upright post and surrounding them with sticks and other inflammable material. Once again it was the duty of the local hangman to carry out the sentence and if he was in a lenient mood he would quietly and quickly pass a wire around the woman's neck and as the flames grew higher a quick tug on the wire and the woman would not feel the flames! Sometimes, especially in the case of heretics, a small bag of gunpowder was placed around the neck or chest and as the flames reached the bag, BANG! But this meant bits of the condemned would be spread around, not nice for the onlookers.

On 31 July 1578 a lady by the name of Maud Whitfield was burned at Bridgnorth for poisoning her husband. And on 23 December 1647 a woman was burned in the Dingle, Shrewsbury, for the same offence – that of attempting to dispose of her hubby. In *Haunted Shrewsbury*, a ghost of a young lady appears on the top floor of the W.H. Smith's store that stands at the top of Pride Hill. The lady concerned was known as Bertha and she dates from the early 1300s. In those days when a lady was accused of witchcraft she had to undergo a trial by water, which meant

As this picture shows, sometimes the lady did feel the heat if the executioner was not quick enough!

having arms and legs tied together so that the lady was in the foetal position. A priest was then called to bless the water and once that had occurred she was then tossed into the river. If she sank then she was deemed to be innocent; she was dead because she had drowned but at least she was innocent! However if she rose to the surface then she was found guilty and hoisted out of the river, taken to the highest point of the town walls and there she was burned at the stake. And the highest point of the walls? Exactly where the top floor of WH Smith stands. So our young Bertha is actually the ghost of a lady being roasted for witchcraft, but more importantly she is still showing us where the hot deeds were done.

Another part of the burning sentence would be branding and this would be carried out in the courts in front of the judges. During Edward VI's reign in 1548 it was decreed that: 'Every person not disabled, sick or aged who is found loitering and not seeking work shall be deemed a vagabond and shall be marked by means of a hot iron with the letter 'V''. Any criminal who was tried and found guilty of theft could, at the court's discretion, be branded with the letter 'T'. This brand would be either on the cheek or the fleshy part of the thumb and sometimes the felons would have the brand on their sides or under their armpits.

Branding ceased to be a civilian punishment in 1829 but continued in the armed forces until 1879 where it would be carried out in front of an entire regiment.

HANGED, DRAWN AND QUARTERED

Just the name was enough to send shivers down most peoples spines. Technically it should be known as drawn, hanged and quartered but that doesn't roll off the tongue quite as well, but what was this terrible form of punishment? For a 'normal' murder the offender was hanged; if the miscreant was a nobleman he would be sentenced to be beheaded. The only crime greater than the murder of a person was high treason, which was tantamount to murdering a country, or murdering the king or queen of a country. If that was the case then something more hideous than a normal execution was needed so along came 'HDQ'.

To give you an idea of what happened here are the words from the judge at the Old Bailey when, in 1660, they sentenced Major General Thomas Harrison who was one of the officers who sentenced Charles I to be executed:

That you be led to the place from whence you came, and from thence be drawn upon a hurdle to the place of execution, and then you shall be hanged by the neck and, being alive, shall be cut down, and your privy members to be cut off, and your entrails be taken out of your body and, you living, the same to be burnt before your eyes, and your head to be cut off, your body to be divided into four quarters, and head and quarters to be disposed of at the pleasure of the King's majesty. And the Lord have mercy on your Soul.

Phew!

Not many people were hanged, drawn and quartered in Shrewsbury but we had many body parts arrive from various places in England and these would be paraded around the town preceded by the town crier who would inform all whose arm or leg it was and what they had done, and woe betide anyone who did the same thing in Shrewsbury.

Hanged, beheaded and drawn.

One person who was hanged, drawn and quartered in town was David, Prince of Wales in 1283. He was the younger son of Llewellen the Great who had enjoyed various arguments, across the years with King John and later he carried on his arguments with Henry III. Llewellen died around 1237 and announced that his son David would carry on the arguments but David had other ideas and in 1241 he handed back all the lands that his father had nicked from the king. Five years later David and the Welsh lords named two of Llewellen's grandsons to take over from David. One was Owain and the other was Llewellen *ap* Gruffydd but, as so often happens, arguments were soon rife amongst the two lads and eventually after five years Owain removed himself from the throng and left Llewellen to rule the Welsh lands and create havoc for the English king.

By 1280 King Edward, who was now on the throne, was hearing complaints about the Welsh ruler from both English and Welsh landowners and decided that something had to be done once and for all. The king summonsed Llewellen to a hearing but Llew refused and called his army to arms to march on the king.

Llewellen left his brother, David, in charge at Shrewsbury and moved south but was killed, leaving David in sole charge. David continued the fight for a while but his heart was not really in it and he was eventually taken captive. In 1283 King Edward held his parliament in Shrewsbury to decide the fate of this Welsh lad. The Shrewsbury Parliament was the first to contain commoners and is the forerunner of today's House of Commons as we know it. The king ordered twenty towns to send deputies and the sheriff of each shire was to provide two knights. This court decided that David was guilty of treason and other crimes ranging from being a traitor to committing a murder on Palm Sunday!

His punishment was to be dragged through the town tied to the tail of a horse (A punishment reserved for knights) and then to be hanged, drawn and quartered at the high cross, which still stands at the top of Pride Hill.

Once the execution had occurred, David's body quarters were sent to Bristol, York,

Winchester and Northampton and his head was taken south where it was put on display at the Tower of London. A plaque, on the wall of Barclay's Bank at the top of Pride Hill, still relates the story to visitors.

One visitor, or part of a visitor, we had in Shrewsbury was Andrew Harcla who was the Earl of Carlisle. The earl had his own army consisting of up to 2,000 men and in 1322 King Edward II requested all his knights to provide men for a battle against the Scots at the Abbey of Eyland. For reasons best known to himself Andrew decided that he would rather spend time with his mates at the local pub and refused to send his army off to fight, a decision he would regret pretty rapidly! Edward lost the battle at Eyland and, needing a scapegoat, he put the blame squarely on the head of Andrew, a head that was to be parted from the rest of him in 1323.

Andrew, Earl of Carlisle was hanged, drawn and quartered at Carlisle Castle. Part of his body was put on display from the highest tower in Carlisle and the rest was sent to Newcastle-upon-Tyne, York and Shrewsbury where it was put on display at the top of Pride Hill before being moved to the castle. His head was treated like any other criminal who received the sentence of 'HDQ' – it was part boiled in a mixture of spices, cumin seeds (to stop the birds pecking at it), water and vinegar before it was then stuck on a pole above London Bridge.

After Edward II died and Edward III took over, Andrew's sister requested that the late earl's body be returned for proper burial. The king agreed and all the bits, including the head, were returned and buried in the family vault.

Who's next?

9

HANGINGS

On 19 April 1777 Jeffery William was hung at Old Heath on the northern outskirts of Shrewsbury for horse stealing and house breaking. A pamphlet costing 2d gives all particulars of his long days of crime and finishes with these calming words: 'The prisoner made such a godly end that it greatly comforted the audience that was innumerable'. It might have comforted the audience but they were not the ones having a rope put around their necks!

If you take the main road out of Shrewsbury, known locally as St Michael's Street, and aim for the A49 you will pass through a locality called Ditherington. This is now a large housing estate and on the left-hand side is the old flax mill, the first iron-framed building in the world.

Below the mill stands the Arriva bus station and it was on this site that a small prison was erected. Prisoners who had been sentenced to be hanged at Old Heath would spend their last day in this prison before being led out to walk the half-mile to the gibbet. The local name for shaking or walking slowly is to dither and there is a belief amongst some people, including me, that the name of the area was Dithering Town shortened to Ditherington, so when the prisoner was led out he would 'dither'.

It has long been believed that the gallows stood on what is now a traffic island close to a supermarket but recent letters have been found that suggest the gallows stood in a completely different spot. Here is a newspaper article dated 26 February 1892:

> The spot where executions formerly took place at Old Heath has been pointed out to me by old residents who have received it from eye witnesses now long since deceased. It [the gallows] is on a bank on the south side of, and near to, Bow-Brook in the field which lies at the back of Gladstone Terrace to the right of the lane leading from Ditherington to the Kennels about 50 yards from the railway bridge. To this place the condemned criminals were brought from the Gaol in carts to be executed. Mr Randles' field on the north side of Bow-Brook is often called Hangman's Croft from it's proximity to the place of execution.

Local tradition says that in the adjoining field was a large pond, bricked around, and that a man stole some ducks from the pond and was branded on his hands as a punishment for his theft. As in most, if not all, other places in the country, the condemned person's body would be left to hang until it literally fell to bits unless the immediate family could pay to have the body handed over to them for burial.

Hangings were commonplace there from the early 1700s until 10 August 1793 when four persons were hung for burglary. Thereafter executions were held on the flat roof of the county goal.

It is recorded that a William Sheynton, thief, was hanged at Kingsland on 31 January 1574 upon a new gallows erected there but before that time people were hung in the town centre itself, probably the square, but there is evidence that during the 1500s the executions took place near to the scene of the crime: on 3 February 1582 John Presetedge was hanged on a gibbet by the side of the abbey mill by the Stone (English) bridge and hung there for three days.

It was also standard practice for a local journalist to visit the condemned man and pen his last words. These were either printed as handbills and sold on the morning of the execution, normally for 1d, or printed in the local paper, *Eddowes Journal*, and later *The Shrewsbury Chronicle*.

It's not really certain if these words were just the prisoner's or whether it's a bit of poetic licence on the part of the journalist but either way the prisoner never got a cut or percentage of the profits!

So let us now delve into the records of the Borough of Shrewsbury and Atcham and *The Shrewsbury Chronicle* to see what sort of people were led to the gallows. Where possible I have tried to list the names of the jury and other officers of the court that attended these cases for those who are researching their family trees – who knows you might even find that it was one of your ancestors that has been left blowing in the wind. But don't worry, I won't tell a soul …

10

SQUIRE SMALLMAN

Judges:
Sir James Allan Park
Sir James Parke

The Grand Jury:
The Hon. Thomas Kenyon, Foreman
Sir E.J. Smythe Bart
Sir R.C. Hill Knight
William Charlton Esq.
John Wingfield Esq.
W. Ormsby Gore Esq.
Thomas Harries Esq.
T. Bulkeley Owen Esq.
A.W. Corbet Esq.
F.K. Leighton Esq.
J.V. Lovatt Esq.
T.N. Parker Esq.
Thomas Eyton Esq.
Thomas Beale Esq.
H.P.T. Aubrey Esq.
Edward Dymock Esq.
Thomas Bayley Esq.
T. Edwards Esq.
G.J. Scott Esq.
Philip Charlton Esq.
Robert Jenkins Esq.
F.B. Harries Esq.

The squire's actual name was John Evans who was a miller by trade, following in his father's footsteps. He was born just over the border in Herefordshire but moved with his parents to the Bishops Castle area of Shropshire. His early schooling was very basic and he soon left education, supposedly to help his father, but he was soon spotted in the company of a local poacher and it was not long before the constabulary was on first-name speaking terms with him!

From poaching he graduated to burglary and then moved on to highway robbery and even did a bit of pick-pocketing just to keep his hand in! He was also a smasher or utterer of coins, the old term of plain forgery, busy lad. He was well travelled in his chosen career having visited Herefordshire, Radnorshire, Shropshire and Montgomeryshire.

Most of the time he was caught and imprisoned in these counties but managed to escape from the prisons, even going to Liverpool for a short time, changing his looks and spending some while being paid to pass around handbills describing his own antics and offering a reward for his capture! Trips to London, Birmingham, Gloucester, Bristol and Ludlow for money forgery followed soon after. John even had time to join the 2nd Brigade of Guards and two other regiments, all of which he deserted from but only after he had made himself a bit of money and stolen some of the regiments' horses which he sent home to Bishops Castle for his own private use.

At the time of his death John was but twenty-eight years of age but the proceeds of his many and various crimes had allowed him to buy and keep horses and hounds and a large house. He was welcomed into the nobility of Shropshire and Herefordshire, gaining the title of squire.

How did the squire find himself on the end of a rope in Shrewsbury? John committed a crime across the border in Herefordshire and was captured but he managed to escape his jailers and made his way back to Bishops Castle. A few days after his escape John visited one of the local pubs in Bishops Castle but was recognised by Edward Richards, who was one of the squire's original captors in Herefordshire. John tried to make his escape but Richards followed him out of the pub calling for help as he went. The squire must have realised that imminent escape was impossible and, turning to face Richards in the street, drew a pistol and shot him at almost point-blank range, seriously wounding him.

The locals from the pub jumped on the squire and held him until the local officer of the law arrived who promptly took him to Shrewsbury. At his trial, which was not a long one, when asked if he would like to say anything in his favour, John admitted his many crimes but wanted

Print from an old leaflet in Shrewsbury Archives No. 665/4/601.

the judge to know that he had never harmed anyone physically, until now. This had little effect on the judge and the death sentence was handed down. In his prison cell John got itchy feet once more and made plans to make an attempt at escaping but this was thwarted by one of the prison officers by the name of Griffiths who sat all night with John and helped him to prepare himself for the following morning. This John did even so far as asking his sister, who visited him on his final night, to return a pistol he had stolen to its rightful owner!

On Saturday 4 April 1829, Evans received holy sacraments from the padre at 11 a.m. The under sheriff of the county postponed the hanging for an hour as a petition had been lodged but as no directive arrived to cancel the punishment he gave his permission and John was then led onto the gallows staging. After publicly confessing his sins to the large crowd gathered and imploring for the mercy of heaven, the bolt was drawn, and Squire Smallman was 'launched into eternity'. After his death his body was handed to his family and friends for internment in an unmarked grave in St Mary's Church, Shrewsbury.

THE LAST WORDS OF SQUIRE SMALLMAN

All you that have a feeling heart,
Give here to what I say,
And by my sad disgraceful end,
Avoid my evil way.

I am a miller by my trade,
Must meet my awful fate,
And the robberies I did commit,
They are in number great.

The hour is come that I must die,
For cruelty and blood,
For I have broken Grievously,
The laws of man and God.

So now a farewell vain world adieu,
Soon will my sorrow cease,
And may I meet my saviour dear,
To dwell with him in bliss.

11

A POACHER CUT DOWN IN HIS PRIME

6 April 1833

Judges:
Mr Justice J. Parke
Mr Justice Taunton

Grand Special Jury:
Sir R.C. Hill, Knight
Thomas Dicken Esq.
James Eakin Esq.
Thomas Evans Esq.
William Howard Esq.
John Jasper Esq.
John Meredith Esq.
John H. Walford Esq.
Mr A. Dodson
Mr T. Ellis
Mr R. Houlding
Mr W. Lloyd

In the 1800s poaching was regarded as a hanging offence and perpetrators of this crime got short shrift with just about any judge, especially if the poacher was found to have perpetrated his crime on land owned by one of the judge's friends.

In 1832 Sir Edward Blount owned the vast majority of the area around Cleobury Mortimer, in south Shropshire. As you can imagine Sir Edward employed a vast amount of staff and one of these was John Bannock who was his head gamekeeper. John's local pub was the Cross Keys in Cleobury (pronounced Clibury), and in November of 1832 John spotted two brothers, William and John Handley, who were known to be keen poachers. Another man who was later identified as Thomas Jones accompanied William and John. The Handleys realised that Bannock may be in the pub for some time and decided to have a bit of sport with some pheasants they knew to be around, and left the pub to collect their tools of the trade – two guns and some sticks. John Bannock, seeing them go, realised what they were up to and also left the pub to raise some of the ground staff. Bannock and his group of men first went to a known favourite cover called 'Peggy's Hole' and after waiting there for a while thought that they may have been mistaken and returned to the manor house to continue their drinking. A little after midnight John heard the sound of a shot coming from another cover called the 'Shoulder of Mutton' and, rousing the staff again, set off to apprehend the poachers. The Shoulder of Mutton was so called because of its shape and the Handleys and Jones had been there for some time. William had shot and killed a hen pheasant and Jones had placed it in a bag when Bannock and his men arrived. Bannock now found himself trapped between the two brothers. The two had decided beforehand that if they were discovered they would impersonate the cry of a sheep so when one of the brothers shouted 'Baa' and the other replied, John turned to face the second man and saw him raise his gun and fire ... John Bannock was hit in the face by thirty-three pellets with four or five landing in his right eye causing him to be permanently blinded. On being hit he cried out, 'Lord I have been hit'.

On hearing John's cry the three poachers did a runner and Thomas Jones, when cross-examined in court, admitted that he had thrown the bag with the pheasant and the sticks over a fence and as part of his defence he stated that he had heard William say that he would, 'prefer to shoot rather than be arrested'.

The prosecution called eight other witnesses as well as Jones who all gave evidence against the brothers, William in particular. Thomas Jones and John Handley were both found not guilty by the jury and were acquitted by the judge, but William was found guilty of attempted murder. After the jury had given its verdict the judge turned to William:

William Handley, the awful moment has arrived when it becomes my painful duty to inform you that your life must be forfeited. You have been found guilty by an impartial jury of a most heinous offence, that of attempting to destroy the life of a fellow creature. It is only the Providence of God that has saved you from having united the crime of murder with your other sins. It makes my heart sick to tell a young man like you in the bloom of health and

The old shire hall once stood in the square and was the scene of many trials.

in the figure of youth that in a few moments you must be no more. Let me implore you to prepare yourself for death. You will receive that spiritual assistance which is essential to your unhappy condition.

William Handley was executed at Shrewsbury Prison on the morning of Saturday 6 April 1833 aged just twenty-nine years of age. A reporter from the *Salopian Journal* wrote:

His fate should be a warning to other desperadoes who have for some time infested this and other counties, and so often add to the crowded state of our prisons. Those who persue the profitless and dangerous practice of poaching are led on to other crimes until as in the present instance their lives become forfeited.

LAST WORDS OF WILLIAM HANDLEY

O God now my last hour has come,
Support me by thy power,
When I ascend to meet my doom,
In that distressing hour.

Most gracious God that's just yet kind,
With pity look on me,
And grant that I may mercy find,
Though on the gallows tree.

And when I reach that happy shore,
Where saints immortal dwell,
O let me praise thee ever more,
And of thy mercy tell.

12

THREE NECKS FOR TWO CHICKENS

4 August 1828

Assize Judges:
Mr Justice Gaselee
Baron Vaughan

Jury:
Lord Viscount Clive, Foreman
T.W.W. Browne Esq.
Edward Cludde Esq.
William Charlton Esq.
Phillip Charlton Esq.
J. Whitehall Dod Esq.
Thomas Eyton Esq.
John Edwards Esq.
J.S. Edwardes Esq.
Thomas Harries Esq.
Francis, K. Leighton Esq.
T. Whitmore MP
W. Whitmore Esq. MP
Sir E.J. Smythe, Bart
P. Corbett Esq. MP
R.W. Smyth Owen Esq.
John Wingfield Esq.
William Tayleur Esq.
T. Bulkeley Owen Esq.
Robert Jenkins Esq.
Peter Broughton Esq.
Benjamin Flounders Esq.
T.C. Whitmore Esq.

Set practically halfway between Shrewsbury and Stafford is the small market town of Market Drayton. Nowadays the town boasts a wonderful marina and boatyard where in the summer months hundreds of people descend on the canals. It is also the home to Muller foods where the yoghurts come from! Back in the early nineteenth century crime was rife in the area thanks mainly to one family, the Coxs. Head of the Cox mafia was sixty-year-old John Cox, a local shoemaker, and his two right-hand men, John Cox junior aged sixteen, and Robert, aged nineteen. They also had other hired help, henchmen Joseph Pugh, aged nineteen, Thomas Ellison aged twenty-three, James Harrison aged twenty-one and Ann Harris aged sixty.

As in a lot of cases the outset of this tale is so simple but the ending is much more horrendous. William Jervis was a landowner of Prees, north Shropshire, and in June of 1828 he discovered the loss of two of his prize chickens. A few days later, on 26 June, Thomas Ellison was apprehended for the crime as he had been implicated on a previous crime of sheep stealing with another man, James Harrison. Prior to the first court appearance regarding the stealing of sheep, Harrison had disappeared before he could be called as a witness and it was thought that he had been approached by the other members of the gang and had decided to lay low for a while. As he was to be the main, and in fact only, witness against Thomas Ellison and could not be found, Thomas was released.

On this second occasion Thomas Ellison informed the constable and the magistrate's clerk that Harrison had been murdered and that his body could be found outside Market Drayton and, if he were allowed his freedom, he would give the names of others connected with the crime. When the constable questioned Thomas further he implicated another two people, Joseph Pugh and Ann Harris, who were promptly arrested, but when they went to the spot that Ellison had marked, no body could be found; Ann was released but Joseph Pugh was detained on suspicion. Pugh then asked to see the clerk himself and made a confession regarding the murder of the informer Harrison.

When Pugh was arrested he in turn named more of his associates – John Cox senior, his son John Cox junior and Robert Cox. Pugh also led the police to the field and showed them where Harrison had been buried. After careful excavation the police found Harrison's body some 5ft down in the earth but by the shape of the body they surmised that the hole had not been big enough to take it. When the body had been put in the earth it was so short that the head had been stuffed up against the chest at a very unusual angle. His right arm and shoulder had also been forced into the hole at a funny angle.

Harrison's clothing was still on him and although it had started to rot away there was enough material still intact to identify him, which was handy as the local surgeon had said that the body was in such a poor state he could not identify the body as Harrison. On finding the body, the Coxs and Ann Harris were all arrested, and although Robert attempted to flee he was caught after he attempted to hide in a field of corn. Once all the players in this act had been caught, the story then began to unfold itself. Harrison had been staying at the home of John Pugh, Joseph's father, but sleeping conditions were extremely poor and when the elder Pughs had retired Joseph and Harrison stayed up in front of the fire. In the early hours of the morning a shrill whistle was heard and John sent his wife, who was eight months pregnant, to see what the commotion was about! Mrs Pugh saw John Cox standing outside the house and a few moments later the two lads from downstairs joined him and all three set off into the moonlight. After a mile or so Joseph suddenly pushed Harrison to the ground and John held him tight whilst Joseph put a rope around Harrison's neck and twisted the rope until Harrison was dead. It was said that Ann Harris had left a shovel outside her house and Robert had collected it for the purpose of burying Harrison's body. An inquest was held locally on 30 June and it transpired that one of the defendants, Ann Harris, was in fact James Harrison's mother by an earlier marriage. This, however, failed to impress the coroner, Mr Joseph Dickin, and after eight hours of questions it transpired that all the witnesses were related in some way and had no problem, laying the blame at each others feet. In fact Pugh told of how he had heard that the Coxs were planning on throwing Harrison into a coal pit or even hiring an assassin to slit his throat!

In the end it transpired that Ann had promised to pay John Cox junior 50s to kill the poor unfortunate informer Harrison. After not too much deliberation the coroner pronounced his verdict – wilful murder against John Cox senior aged sixty, John Cox junior aged thirty-five, Robert Cox aged nineteen and Ann Harris aged fifty, all of Market Drayton, and Joseph Pugh aged nineteen of Little Drayton. All five were transported to Shrewsbury Prison to be tried for murder.

At 8 a.m. on Wednesday 30 July the court began its trial. The judges for this 'much talked about' trial were Judge Stephen Gaselee and Judge Baron Vaughan. It was a long trial and did not finish until just before midnight when the foreman of the jury at last pronounced their findings – guilty of the murder of James Harrison against Joseph Pugh, John Cox junior and Robert Cox.

The jury found Ann Harris and John Cox senior guilty of being an 'accessory before the fact'. Ann and John Cox senior's sentence did not carry an immediate death sentence like the other three.

On Monday 4 August 1828, Joseph Pugh and John Cox junior were led out onto the platform above Shrewsbury Goal and were hanged alongside another criminal, William Steventon, who had been found guilty at another trial of the murder of John Horton (see Death of a Sergeant).

After the men had hung for the regulation one hour their bodies were cut down and local people were allowed to have the dead men's hands placed on them! This was supposed to be a local cure for 'Wens', a type of arthritis. The bodies of John Pugh and William Steventon were taken to the Salop Infirmary (now a shopping centre and flats) for dissection and John Cox's body was sent to Market Drayton for the same purpose. For some reason Robert Cox had been given a reprieve and he managed to fade into obscurity.

On Saturday 16 August 1828 Ann Harris was led out onto the same platform above the main gate of Shrewsbury Goal at midday to face the long drop. This she did on her own as old John Cox had also been reprieved, but the padre reported that she had given her life to God early that morning and went to meet her maker with a light heart, although she still claimed that old John Cox was as guilty as her.

The local newspaper reported that over 5,000 people attended the hanging of Ann, not just because she was female but because she was the first woman to be hung for over twenty years. This was such a heinous crime of murder against a fellow human that merely the theft of two chickens had set the judicial ball rolling.

LAST WORDS OF ANN HARRIS

With groans and sighs I draw my breath,
And trembling waits the hour of death,
Oh Christ show mercy I call to thee,
Now I'm brought to the fatal tree.

Condemned this awful death to die,
I look onto the Lord most high,
Aloud to him for mercy call,
Hoping that he will save my soul.

Oh Lord who's awful thunders roll,
Turn; oh turn my hardened soul,
Turn me onto Christ and thee,
The holy undivided trinity.

Hark the heavy clanging chains,
Eternity on time now gains,
A dear eternity in bliss to dwell,
Or howl eternity in hell.

Oh that I could call back the time,
That I committed such a crime,
Which brought me here in chains confined,
And soon must leave this world behind.

May death through Jesus be my friend,
May death be light when life doth end,
Crown my last moments withy thy power,
The latest in the latest hour.

Thousands arrived in Shrewsbury to
see Ann hang, the first women to be
hung in twenty years.

Hark the solemn prison bell,
That tolls my destiny to tell,
Hark distant feet they come to tell,
That I am called to die.

Then farewell friends and earthly cares,
My mortal race is over and run,
Great God accept my dying prayers,
Through thy most dear and blessed son.

13

WHERE RELIGION AND MURDER MET AT CLUN

June 1633

During the early seventeenth century, England was going through a religious turmoil as the various kings and queens on taking up residence changed the doctrines according to their wishes: Protestants, Catholics, Papists etc. There was even an Act of Uniformity whereby everyone was made to attend church on a Sunday and were fined up to 1s each if they failed to attend, and that included the servants as well!

One of the landowners in the Clun area of south Shropshire was Edward *ap* Evans and he had two sons and five daughters. Unfortunately the daughter's names are not forthcoming but they do not figure much in this tale, it is the sons and the mother who were the main characters. The family were deeply religious and, as was their wont, would spend a certain amount of time every day reading from the family Bible and praying for the area. One of the sons, Enoch, was the eldest of the two boys, the other being John, and although Enoch had not had much education he was able to read well and owned his own Bible which he would take into the fields or the barn with him and read when there were a spare few minutes. Enoch had his own ideas about religion and would often refuse to kneel to accept the communion bread and wine saying that kneeling stopped the priest's blessings and the sacraments reaching his legs!

On one Sunday at their local church, as the vicar, Erasmus Powell, offered Enoch the chalice Enoch roared at him to fill the chalice to the brim which the frightened vicar did with great alacrity and Enoch downed the lot in one gulp!

On another occasion in mid-winter Enoch was found totally naked lying face down in a running stream by a very surprised and shocked newly married couple and they persuaded him to put his trousers on and return home.

Enoch and John were like most other brothers of that time, sharing most things, so it was no surprise that they owned land and cattle together but John was quite upset at some of the dark religious moods that Enoch regularly got into.

Things came to a head when John and his mother, Joan, decided that Enoch had to be spoken to regarding his refusal to kneel at the communion rail and on Saturday 13 June 1633 a right old ding dong of an argument took place between the three of them which resulted in Enoch (in John's words at the time) 'becoming very rude to our mother and storming out of the house'.

Hung in chains.

Things quietened down a little and on 4 July the same year Enoch travelled to Knighton, three miles from his home, to visit a Margaret Jones whom he had plans to marry. Margaret seems to have agreed to Enoch's advances and promised to meet him at a local public house where they would plan their marriage. Enoch returned home and settled down to sleep but was so excited that at around 1 a.m. he woke his brother John and they both dressed after which John agreed to accompany Enoch to the pub that very minute.

They both set off but to Enoch's disappointment, and anger, Margaret failed to turn up at the agreed time and to add insult to injury had sent a message saying that the wedding was off and that she did not wish to see Enoch ever again. The two men returned home, Enoch in a foul mood and John impatient to return to his fields.

John was a man who lived by only a few rules and, as was his normal custom when coming in from the fields around midday, had a small meal and then settled down for a short nap,

Enoch knew of John's ritual and for some unknown reason he found a sharp hand axe or hatchet and on entering the kitchen struck John across the neck. The first blow stunned John but as he rose to ward Enoch away his brother struck again, and this time John's head came off and rolled across the floor!

The boy's mother, Joan, heard the commotion and rushed into the kitchen to find bits of John on different parts of the floor and as she turned to remonstrate with her other son, Enoch struck at her as well. It seems that Enoch was not a good aim because, as with his brother, the first attack went wrong and Joan made a grab for him and hung on tight but Enoch then stabbed her three or four times in the chest, killing her. He then dragged her body towards the door and for good measure cut her head off as well!

He then locked the door, washed the two heads with clean water and wrapped them in a shirt before placing them on the kitchen table. After he had smashed a hole in the wall to make it appear as if there had been an intruder, Enoch went to his room and changed out of his blood soaked things into clean clothes. He then returned to the kitchen, collected the two heads and hid them in the log pile. He then walked about two miles to a relative's house and on finding that his cousin was out, sat and read a passage from his Bible, the first chapter of Isaiah.

When his cousin returned the following day Enoch asked him to accompany him back to his house, and the cousin agreed. By this time Edward, the father, had returned from Bishops Castle market to find the two headless bodies of his wife and son. On finding Enoch missing he called the local constabulary who found the son walking home with his cousin. At first Enoch denied any knowledge of the crime but then asked for the minister Erasmus Powell to be present.

As soon as the minister arrived Enoch immediately admitted his guilt and the small party of police and the accused started to walk the eighteen miles to Shrewsbury. Passing his father's house, Enoch asked to see his him but his dad refused and the group carried on. As night fell they were forced to spend the night at the Round House in Pulverbatch before continuing to Shrewsbury.

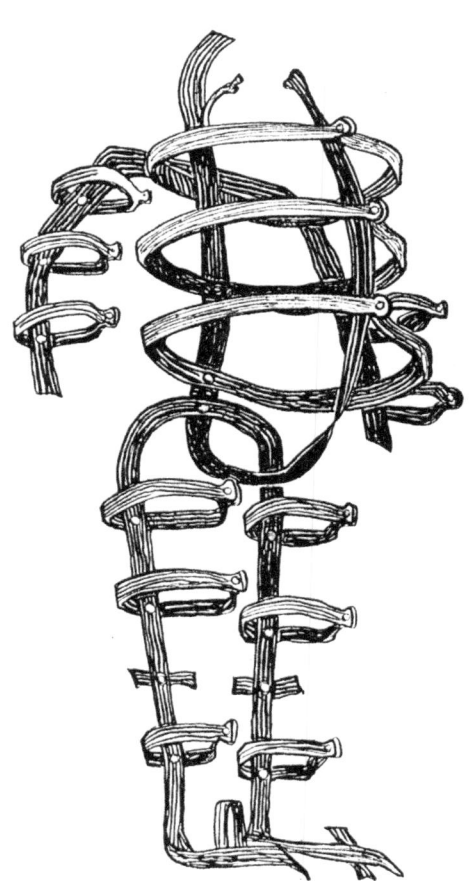

They arrived in the county town on Sunday 7 July and the court sat on the Monday morning. After a very short trial the jury in Shrewsbury found Enoch guilty of the two murders and the judge ordered that he should be taken to a spot near to where the murders had been committed and be 'Hung in Chains' on the gibbet.

The gibbet was not really to hang felons by the neck until dead but to hang them in a cage-like device or just wound with chains and left to die, normally about three days.

Enoch's sisters hired an army soldier, Hugh Meredith, and another young man to cut Enoch down a few days after he had died and they buried him in a pit close to their father's house and although they admitted what they had done, they were released without charge.

14

THE MURDER OF A VILLAGE CHILD

1867

Nowadays most people's idea of a prisoner in jail is that of a hardened felon who has no feelings, but when a criminal is jailed for a crime against a child then even the most hardened of men can find themselves meeting out some form of punishment on the perpetrator, on the quiet of course.

And so it turned out that even the normal, law-abiding villagers of Longden found themselves on a manhunt in the later part of 1867.

Nine-year-old Catherine Lewis was a well-liked young lady in this village not ten miles from Shrewsbury and often helped out at various events in different houses. The Davies family owned one of the houses she worked in and she would often act as the servant and regularly went to church with the family. On one Sunday all was as normal and Catherine accompanied the family to church as usual. Mrs Davies recalled pinning a small brooch on Catherine's shawl to keep it tight and help keep the cold out. Catherine also wore a straw hat with coloured ribbons around the brim.

After the service Catherine, along with a young servant girl and three or four other younger children, all set out for their various homes accompanied by a local farm labourer, John Mapp. John was in his early thirties and, although he had a past record of an assault on a young woman and been sentenced to transportation, everyone thought he had turned over a new leaf on his return but, as we shall see, it was not to be.

At various road junctions along the way the young members of the group bade their farewells to each other until only John and Catherine were left, and that was the last time she was ever seen alive. Knowing that Catherine often stayed with the Davies family overnight her parents were not unduly worried that she did not return home, and it was only when a young waggon boy found her straw hat covered in blood the next day that her father begin a search of the surrounding area.

The first person he saw on the road was John Mapp who was working in a nearby field and on asking if John had seen the girl his reply was no. Catherine's father carried on his search and later on, as the light was beginning to fade, he spotted a barn that was owned by a Shrewsbury man by the name of Jones, and entered. After a short search of the lower floor in which he found nothing unusual he then climbed a ladder and found the bloodstained body of his daughter in the hayloft.

Naturally in a state of shock, Mr Lewis ran out of the barn and spotted two local men returning from their labours in the field. After they had understood what the unfortunate father had found, they agreed to enter the hayloft and stand guard over the poor girl's body whilst the father fetched the local constable.

The constable immediately began making his enquiries and after a whole host of witnesses came forward, and speaking to the group of youngsters from the church, John Mapp was soon listed as the main suspect for Catherine's murder and was duly arrested.

At the trial, held in Shrewsbury, it was discovered that John, after the other members of the group had left them, had walked with Catherine along a lane and had, at some point, picked up a large branch and struck Catherine across the back of her head before cutting her throat with his knife. For some unexplainable reason, it was not to quieten her for she was obviously dead from the throat wound, Mapp pushed part of Catherine's shawl into her mouth. Mapp then pushed her body into a ditch for the night before returning early the next morning to drag the poor girl into the barn. When the constable searched Mapp, Catherine's brooch was found in his pocket – damning evidence indeed.

Giving evidence, John Mapp agreed that he had owned a knife but had left it in his house. The blood found on his clothing was put down to John suffering a nosebleed and the brooch

One of the only portraits of Calcraft taken on his retirement as public hangman.

had been bought from a man in the local pub, but John could not identify him. Mapp stated that after he and the girl had said farewell to everyone they had walked on for a short while before she had turned off for her own house.

All the evidence against John Mapp mounted up, even John's father stated that Mapp was in bed early, so how could he have been to the local pub to buy a brooch?

It took the jury just six minutes to return a verdict of murder and the judge passed down the normal sentence. No-one knows even today what happened, certainly no molestation of the girl was found to have occurred. Was it just his past catching up with him through something that Catherine may have said or asked? Sadly we shall never know because John Mapp went to the gallows full of remorse but still tight-lipped about what happened on the road from Longden.

John Mapp was executed by the infamous William Calcraft and this was Calcraft's only recorded visit to Shrewsbury.

15

FIVE HIGHWAYMEN AT LOPPINGTON

March 1836

The judge at the trial was Mr Justice Littledale and the grand jury were:

The Hon. Robert Henry Clive of Oakley Park
The Hon. Thomas Kenyon of Prado
Sir Baldwin Leighton of Loton, Bart
Sir Ferdinand Richard Acton of Aldenham, Bart
Sir Edward Joseph Smythe of Acton Burnell, Bart
Sir Rowland Hill, of Hawkstone, Bart
Sir Robert Chambre Hill of Prees, KCB
John Roger Kynaston of Hardwick, Esq.
John Cotes of Woodcote, Esq.
Thomas Netherton Parker of Sweeney, Esq.
John Michael Severne of Wallop, Esq.
Joseph Venables Lovatt of Belmont, Esq.
Thomas Botfield of Hopton Court, Esq.
John Davies, of Merrington Hall, Esq.
Thomas Henry Hope of Netley, Esq.
William Owen of Woodhouse, Esq.
Thomas Whitmore of Apley Park, Esq.
William Wolryche Whitmore of Dudmaston, Esq.
Edward Cludde of Orleton, Esq.
Henry Pinson Tozer Aubrey of Broom Hall, Esq.
Francis Blythe Harries of Benthall, Esq.

Counsel for the prosecution were Mr Bather and Mr Lee and the solicitor was Mr Moore of Shrewsbury. Counsel for the prisoners were Mr Watson and Mr Meteyard and the solicitor was Mr Penny from Shrewsbury.

The word 'highwayman' immediately brings to mind a character like Dick Turpin, robbing rich men on the roads around London whilst smiling at the ladies in the carriage and then racing back on his horse to his lady friends, but in Shropshire it wasn't so dramatic.

Thomas Woodward was a highly respected businessman in Shrewsbury, a malt miller by trade. On 23 March 1836 he travelled to Wrexham in the company of Thomas Urwick who was his nephew. After finishing his business transactions in the Welsh town, Woodward and his nephew set of for home around 3 p.m. arriving in Ellesmere about 6 p.m. and after a change of horses set off again around 6.45 p.m. Thomas Urwick was driving and around 7.30 p.m., as they approached the little hamlet of Wackley near Loppington, the horse was spooked by something lying in the road. As the nephew tried to steer around the blockage two men suddenly sprang out of the ditch on one side of the road and three others came from behind the carriage.

Thinking that the men were drunk Mr Woodward decided to sit still but when he turned to his nephew to advise him to do the same he received a blow to the head that knocked him out for a while. As he came to he saw three of the men take hold of the gig and they began to tip it over, spilling both the Shrewsbury men out into the road. The robbers then proceeded to take all Mr Woodward's money which was a £10 note, a £5 note, around eight sovereigns, 19s in silver, and a silk pocket handkerchief. Thomas Urwick lost four half crowns and some silver as well as a fob watch. The robbers then made off and the two attacked men made for a nearby house.

Who were the attackers? Originally the gang consisted of eight men from Ireland. They were well known in and around the county of Shropshire as well as being known across the length and breadth of Wales. Technically they followed the trade of pig-drovers but as we will see this was their cover.

The McDaniels, Patrick, Owen and Edward led the gang. All three men were well educated and Patrick and Owen took on the role of leadership whilst Edward looked after the finances. The other two men concerned in this attack were Lawrence Curtis who was also known as Lawrence McGuire and John Mullholland also known as John Holland.

Both these last two men were, in the words of the McDaniels, 'ignorant and knowing nothing'. Patrick had been working in and around the Welsh borders for twelve years and was described as 'coldly calculating and extremely harsh'. Owen was similar to his brother but more of a humorous character owning property in Ireland. Edward McDaniel was also known as Donnelly and was a hard man who would not hesitate to strike anyone who got in his way. He was married and had three children who all lived in a small town called Bulbriggan nearly eighteen miles from Dublin. Lawrence was also a hard man but was the first to offer evidence against the others in the hope that he would be given a lighter sentence, and the last man John Mullholland or Holland was the youngest member of the gang in as much as he had only recently joined them from his home in Bulbriggan, the same town as McDaniel, where he also had a wife and four children.

In the attack on the two men near Loppington, it was Patrick and John who approached from the ditch with Patrick grabbing the horse's head and holding it under his arm. The first blow to Woodward's head was struck by Curtis (McQuire) and it was Edward, McDaniel and Curtis who tipped the gig over. All five men made good their escape and things would have settled down had it not been for the fact that the men were arrested in Manchester just one week later for another crime that they had committed.

When they were handed over to Mr Richard Green, the warden of Manchester Gaol, Curtis asked to see the superintendent of Manchester police, Mr Joseph Sadler. Thomas was admitted to Mr Saddler's office in the early hours of the morning saying that he wanted to make a statement admitting to the crime at Wackley. After the superintendent had cautioned him, Mr Sadler called for two constables to act as witnesses; Curtis then gave a full confession and named the other four men who were with him:

> I was present at the robbery of two men in a gig on the road between Ellesmere and Shrewsbury, Patrick caught hold of the horse and Thomas, Edward and myself took hold of the gig and tipped the two men out onto the road. Thomas took the watch and the McDaniels took the money, I believe about twenty-five pounds. The notes were changed in Chester.

After Curtis had given his confession he was returned to the cells where he told the others what he had done; the jailers then moved him to another cell for his own safety. Mullholland then decided to try and help his own cause and called for the constables to convey him to the office as he wanted to make a statement to the superintendent. When he was cautioned and questioned about the watch, Mullholland stated that it was his and that he had bought it in Stockport but could not remember how much he had paid or from whom he had purchased it.

All five prisoners were brought to Shrewsbury to face the courts on Monday 1 August 1836. At the trial none of the five men had anything to say in their defence – even Curtis and Mullholland were quiet, but numerous witnesses were called to give evidence against them. Mr Thomas Pay, a hostler at the Red Lion, Ellesmere and Mary Copnall who lived opposite the Red Lion, both saw the five men leave in the direction of Loppington; Mr Richard Done had seen the men hiding in the ditch prior to the attack.

Execution of Irishmen. (Courtesy of Shropshire Archives No. 665/4/608)

After hearing the evidence it did not take the jury long to reach a unanimous verdict of 'guilty' against all five men and on accepting the verdict the judge put on the black cap and gazed down on the men in the dock:

You have been found guilty of highway robbery on Mr Thomas Woodward and with assaulting and ill treating him, The law has very properly made your offence a capital crime and when that crime is accompanied with violence like that which you have used in this instance it becomes imperative that the law should be carried out to its fullest extent. Your case is one of the most aggravated I have ever heard of and I feel fully satisfied with the verdict of the jury.

I therefore feel it my duty to make an example of you, for if I do not, others who may hereafter be tempted to commit this crime, will say 'Oh, its only transportation for life, and, therefore, I may take your life or ill-use, as I think proper' You have therefore nothing to hope for in this world. Your plea for mercy must now be directed to the Almighty for your stay in this world will be very short. You, John Mullholland, are the only one to whom I can hold out any hope of commutation, as your conduct seems to have been less atrocious than any of the others, but for them there is no hope. Let me, then, implore you to seek such spiritual assistance as will enable you to prepare for the awful fate which awaits you, that you may repent of your sins and gain forgiveness of Heaven.

The death sentence was then passed.

A LAST MESSAGE FROM THE CONDEMNED MEN

Dear Friends

We write these last few lines to you hoping they may find you in good health, but we are at present very indifferent being confined in these dismal cells, without any light and left to reflect upon those days we spent so happy and cheerful before we entered into those scenes of dissipation which are certain to bring us, and all who follow our example, to an untimely and disgraceful death.
But thanks to the Almighty, we are prepared to meet them in heaven and hope to enjoy eternal life.

So, adieu our friends, for the present.

John Mullholland never received his pardon and on the morning of 13 August 1836 all five men were led out onto the gallows of Shrewsbury Goal and after receiving a short blessing from the prison chaplain the hoods were pulled over their heads and they were 'launched into eternity'.

16

DEATH OF A COLLIER

February 1812

It is often said that 'money is the root of all evil', and you only have to look at the many hundreds if not thousands of executions that have taken place to see that money had a hand in the outcome.

On 1 February 1812 Mr Bailey, a retired collier who lived in Old Park near Wellington, was found dead in a stone quarry close to his house. His injuries were many, including a deep wound on the crown of his head, another over his eyes, two deep gashes across his throat and several fractures to his head. He was sixty-four years old, had no wife or children and lived alone so family feuds were discounted, but after some questioning a local neighbour by the name of John Griffiths was soon placed at the top of the wanted section.

Griffiths lived about a mile from Bailey, was currently working as a cooper and was building himself a new house. It was known that he had a problem with money and had been heard to ask Bailey for a loan on a number of occasions, however the requests had always been denied.

The local constable spoke to witnesses and soon realised that they had their man, and Griffiths was arrested and sent to Shrewsbury to stand trial. The trial was held on Friday 27 March 1812 and lasted for seven hours. Mr Abbott opened the proceedings and the witnesses were questioned by Mr Eyton junior.

The first witness was a young boy who gave evidence that he found the body of Mr Bailey on Saturday 1 February in the stone quarry and he ran to tell others about what he had seen. These witnesses told of how they found the body with a fractured head and his throat cut and although it had been raining that night his clothes were clean and dry. Bailey also had only one shoe on and this was clean as well. There were no blood marks around the body. When questioned, Mrs Elizabeth Bowdler, a neighbour, said that she saw the prisoner drag a parcel up the steps and over the wall of his new house between 8–9 p.m. He left the parcel at the top of the stairs and looked both left and right before dragging his load around the back of the house. When asked how she knew it was Griffiths, she replied that she could see him clearly by the light of the moon and the glow from the flames of Mr Botfield's iron works.

Next to give evidence was Mr Bailey's brother who stated that when he saw his brother in the quarry he found his keys on the ground so he went to his brother's house and on opening the money drawer with the keys he found it empty.

Another neighbour, Mr John Braggs, said that he saw Griffiths coming from the corner of his new house with both hands full of sand but when he saw Braggs the accused dropped the sand and ran indoors.

Constable William Dunning stated that after the body had been found, and on hearing Mrs Bowdler's evidence, he had gone to Griffiths' house and found blood stains on the wall at the top of the steps; there had been an attempt to scrape the wall clean of blood. There were also traces of blood in a cellar along with a shirt hidden under some coal with Mr Bailey's initials on it and a cooper's adze with bloodstains on it. The constable produced a bag containing congealed blood taken from the new house as evidence.

A Mr Samuel Jones assisted Constable Dunning in removing the floorboards of the house and confirmed finding a cellar approximately 8ft x 4ft and about 5ft deep under the floorboards. Finding bloodstains on the floor, he also confirmed that the only way into the cellar was to remove the boards. The high constable, Mr G. Shepherd, then produced the adze with the bloodstains and the shirt as evidence.

Next to give evidence was the local surgeon, Mr G. Evans, who said that he saw the body at the deceased man's house on the Saturday night and described the body having an angular wound over the left eye that must have been given by a heavy instrument. There was also a wound near the crown of the head. The throat had been cut but not the windpipe or the jugular and no important vein had been damaged. The surgeon saw the blood in the house and surmised that it was about the quantity that would have been lost. He stated that the blood could not have been there ten hours because it would have begun to putrefy. The skull was fractured on the right side and this blow alone would be sufficient to cause death. Mr Evans then stated that he removed the deceased's scalp so as to lay the skull bare and compare the wound with the cooper's adze, which was a perfect match; part of the skull was produced for the court to see.

Another surgeon, Mr Webb, was called and he said he examined the body along with Mr Evans and could confirm all that the court had heard.

Next to give evidence were Mr Bailey's two sisters, Elizabeth and Mary, who swore to the shirt being the property of the dead man.

Mr William Rigby said that the prisoner was at his house when a constable called telling of the finding of the body. Mr Rigby then asked Griffiths to go with him but Griffiths replied that he did not like seeing dead bodies.

A Mr Hammersley saw the prisoner on the morning when the body was found and remarked what a shocking murder it was in such a peaceful place. The prisoner replied it was and Mr Hamersley said that he hoped the villains would be found out, to which Griffiths made no reply.

At his examination Griffiths stated that the last time he saw Bailey was on Tuesday 30 January when he, Bailey, asked for some change. Griffiths told the court that he took change for three bills around to Bailey's house that night. He accounted for the blood under the floorboards by saying that he kept some horseflesh with which to feed his dog, and the shirt he stated that he bought from Birmingham two years previously but he could not think how they came to be under the coals. He had ground his adze a few days before but could not think how blood got onto it and he stated that he was working on his new house all day on the Friday. As to the money found on his person, he said that he got that through his trade and mentioned some of the people who had paid him including a printed £5 note from a bank in Shifnal from a Mrs Mary Dunning. Mrs Dunning told the court that she had paid Griffiths with an old printed Shrewsbury bank note and not a Shifnal note about ten weeks before the murder.

Mr Edwards, a local pawnbroker, said that Griffiths had pawned two watches with him, one in October for 20s and one in December for 10s. The prisoner's wife also pawned some clothes that had never been redeemed.

When asked if he would like to question any of the witnesses Griffiths asked that the surgeon Mr Webb be called for. Griffiths then stated that when the body had been brought into the house someone asked Griffiths to touch it and that he put his thumb and forefinger into the wound and that the fracture was no more than a scratch, and that Mr Webb said he thought the fracture could have been caused by falling into the quarry and that there was dirt in the wound. Mr Webb said that at no time did he say that the fracture had been caused by a fall.

After the seven-hour trial the jury quickly returned a verdict of wilful murder and the judge sentenced Griffiths to be hanged at Shrewsbury on the Monday morning.

On the morning of Monday 30 March 1812, John Griffiths was led out onto the staging in front of Shrewsbury Prison. After a few words he asked the spectators to join him in singing a hymn and soon after the singing had finished the hood was pulled over Griffiths' head and he was launched into eternity.

LAST WORDS OF JOHN GRIFFITHS

Rather sit at home and starve at your fire-sides in want that you may die in peace than do anything that will bring you to a prison or a gallows. I wish that it may be life to all those who come to see me die. Many of you are affected at seeing me now but you will soon forget me. O look at me and never forget this scene, do not deceive yourselves, you cannot deceive God, I thought I could deceive him but I have only deceived myself.

I see many faces here whom I know but I hope to meet them again in Heaven.

Gibbet warning.

17

ATTEMPTED MURDER OF A VICAR

March 1819

In any country, to murder someone is just about the worst crime anyone can commit in today's modern world and to attempt a murder is almost as bad, however in the nineteenth century murder or attempted murder carried the same sentence – death by hanging. What made this crime even more newsworthy was the fact that the attempt was on the life of a member of the clergy.

John Denny was sixty-four years old and had traded as an apprentice blacksmith in Longden, about six miles south of Shrewsbury, before being taken into the workhouse in Pontesbury. Denny never knew his own parents but believed that he was born in or around London. As a young child he was brought to live in Osbaston, a small hamlet near Knockin, and then went to live with a Mr Clemson in Moreton near Oswestry. After a short time there he was moved again to the Foundling Hospital in Shrewsbury and stayed there until he gained his apprenticeship in Longden.

In August 1818 Denny was approached by the Revd John Wilde in the workhouse, was told to go out and find some work and given 5s to help him. On 17 August, Denny returned and asked the Revd Wilde if it would be possible to have an order of readmission to the workhouse put on him and offered to return the 5s. The Revd Wilde refused to sign the order and told Denny that he could use the money to keep himself until the next meeting of the parish management committee the next Monday. The following day Denny again applied for readmission and was this time turned down by both the Revd Wilde and Mr Peters, the workhouse manager. Denny turned and walked away. That same evening the Revd Wilde was walking across the courtyard of his house when he was approached by Denny who followed him towards his house. The reverend asked him to leave and Denny replied, raising his voice, 'By God, I will not leave it'.

Fearing for his own safety, the reverend told Denny that he would make him leave and called one of his staff to fetch the local constable whilst he went inside and bolted the door. Later on one of the female staff wanted to leave the house and called on the vicar to open the door for her. As the reverend unbolted the door he saw Denny still out in the courtyard and as soon as Denny spotted him he once more asked for readmission. The reverend once again stated that he could not, nor would not, give Denny the readmission he wanted.

As the reverend was talking, Denny had been slowly moving towards the clergyman and when he was about 2ft from him he again repeated his request and at the same time drew a small dagger from under his coat and stabbed the reverend in the side. At the trial the reverend said that at first he felt no pain but when he returned to his rooms he suddenly felt something warm trickle down his side and on removing his waistcoat and shirt saw blood pumping out of his body.

The Revd Wilde went back out into the courtyard crying 'murder', saw Denny still standing there and called for someone to hold onto him.

After the reverend had given his statement, the next witness to be called was the local blacksmith, Thomas Breeze, who stated that he remembered Denny calling in to his forge and asking if he could use the grinding stone. Breeze then told how he saw Denny take a knife out of his coat and sharpen the point and leading edge for about two minutes. When Breeze asked what he was going to do with the knife Denny replied, 'I shall not tell you, you will hear more about it before night'.

Next to be called was the vestry clerk of Pontesbury, Mr John Stretch. He stated that he saw Denny about ten minutes after he was taken into the constable's custody and asked him if he was ashamed of himself. Denny replied, 'No, I am not ashamed of myself, I would kill a parson as kill a toad'. Stretch stated that Denny appeared to be completely sober.

The local constable, Edward Brown, was called and gave his evidence: 'I seized Denny and told him that he must come with me. Denny asked me if I wanted him and I said yes'. Denny then replied 'I will go anywhere, I would rather be hanged as starved to death. I think it no more harm to kill a parson as kill a toad'.

Another member of the public who had helped the constable, Mr Jones, then said that he also asked Denny if he was ashamed of what he had done and Denny had replied that, 'he was sorry he had not done it quite enough'.

The judge, Sir William Garrow, then asked Denny if he had anything to say in his defence.

Denny replied that he was sorry for what he had done to the reverend but he was intoxicated at the time and had not realised what he was doing.

In his summing up the judge told the court: 'Drunkeness has been used as an excuse in this and many other similar cases' but he hoped that the jury 'would recognize the fact that drink would not help anyone but instead hinder their cause'. He added that at no time had Denny shown any remorse for the crime he had committed and it took the jury just a short time before they reached their verdict: 'Guilty of attempted murder'.

Sir William then passed sentence with these words:

John Denny, after a patient investigation of the circumstances of your case by a very attentive and humane jury you stand convicted of a most heinous crime. Varying from the usual course pursued by me I proceed to pass the sentence upon you at this time and for this I have more than one reason.

I should wish all these who have been present at your trial to know your fate and the consequences to which the commission of crime must inevitably lead. I also wish that you, who have so little time to live should make use of the short period allotted to you in a befitting manner.

I wish you, by contrition, by a total change of mind by having recourse to the precepts of religion and by a reliance on the meditation of a crucified saviour to seek that future peace which Christianity offers to the penitent sinner.

The object of the law in inflicting capital penalties is not merely to punish criminals but to let others know by such examples that the peace of society and the comforts and properties of independents shall not be broken in upon with impunity.

That the prosecutor, (Rev Wilde), is here present and spared to his family and society is not a debt owing to you but to the good providence of a benign and merciful God. You have therefore but a few days to live and I conjure you to make the best use of that short period by having recourse to those religious means I before pointed out to you.

The judge then passed the sentence of death and Denny was led away without saying a word or looking left or right.

On the morning of Saturday 3 April 1819, John Denny was led out onto the gallows at Shrewsbury Prison. He remained silent right to the end.

18

A BUTCHER SCORNED

August 1833

In all of the accounts that I have written about in this book I am indebted to the unknown journalists who worked on *The Shrewsbury Chronicle* and other local papers who wrote the original accounts. Because there was no such thing as photographs in those days these writers had to paint a picture of the events in words and were quite diligent at filling in readers with all the information, until this one! For some unknown reason the journalist failed to give any information about the murdered gentleman but still managed to copy, or write, the last words of the condemned man.

George Hayward was a twenty-year-old butcher who lived in Beckbury, a small village between Wellington and Wolverhampton. On 8 July 1833, Hayward called in to the house of Mr John Causer to see his sister whom Hayward had been courting. Mr Causer's mother was not happy at the courtship between the two and on seeing the young man in her house told Hayward that her daughter was not in and asked him to leave. At first Hayward was not keen to leave but when Mrs Causer called for her son to help get rid of Hayward they both left arguing. A few minutes later John returned to his home bleeding profusely, calling to his mother that he had been stabbed in the belly and he was gone. His mother got him to bed where he died a short while later.

Maria Meeson was Hayward's landlady and at the trial she stated that Hayward came home a short time after 9 p.m. She was in bed but heard him go into the pantry off the kitchen and then go out. Maria got out of bed and looking out of the window saw him walk down the street, and a while later heard an argument taking place. She then heard the sound of a blow and heard Causer cry, 'Oh George what have you done?' and heard Hayward answer 'Jack, I have done the thing that is right'. Maria then heard Hayward return home, go into the pantry and then go to bed.

Two other witnesses were called – Mr William Sutton and Mr Brian Adams. They both stated that they were walking down the street and passed the two men arguing but paid little attention as they thought that they were fooling around. A short while later, as they were sitting in the pub, they heard that Causer had been stabbed and rushed out to see blood oozing from Causer's shirt. They watched him go into his house and then waited for the constable to arrive.

The local surgeon, Mr Fletcher, gave evidence that he was called to Causer's house and saw that he had been stabbed in the belly twice and that the knife had entered his intestines and that either of the stab wounds would have proved fatal.

The surgeon also gave evidence that Hayward owned three knives which he used to eat with and that one of them had blood on it.

Mr Bates, the rector of Beckbury, gave evidence that he had been called to Causer's house and on asking John what had taken place the dying man had told him that he had turned Hayward out of his mother's house and an argument had ensued. Hayward had then told Causer that he 'Would have his rights', and then stabbed John. The rector then said that soon after this John Causer had passed away.

It did not take the jury long to reach a unanimous verdict: guilty of murder – and the judge proceeded to put the traditional black cap on and passed the sentence of death imploring Hayward to spend the rest of his time alive to make peace with his maker who he would soon meet.

On the morning of Monday 5 August 1833, George Hayward received sacrament from the gaol's padre and then made the short walk to the staging above Shrewsbury Prison. As soon as he arrived he spent a few minutes in silent prayer before the hood was pulled over his face, and he was launched into eternity.

LAST WORDS OF GEORGE HAYWARD

O listen to my dying song,
Ye tender mothers dear,
My time on earth cannot be long,
Pale death is drawing near.

Soon must I leave this body here,
Soon must my soul away,
O awful thought my soul prepare,
For that tremendous day.

Remembrance breaks my bleeding heart,
To think on days gone by,
For like an early blossom cast,
In prime of life I die.

Murder is the worst of crimes,
That ever the soul can stain,
And threatened is most certainly,
With everlasting pain.

O how shall I prepare my heart,
Eternal life to gain,

Jesus, thy grace thy strength impart,
    Or all I do is vain.

Now drop a tear fair reader o'er,
    This elegy of mine,
And while your pity works within,
    Abhor the murderers crime.

19

THE IRONBRIDGE RAPIST

3 March 1822

In today's modern world any crime that leads to a court appearance inevitably means a long-drawn-out trial where countless number of witnesses are called by both sides and much argument and counter argument takes place. Various reports on the case are then called for by the defence and the prosecution, however this was not so in the eighteenth and nineteenth centuries.

During that time most criminals were tried and sentenced before they even set foot in a dock and this next report from Mrs Wadeson, a printer in Shrewsbury, left the reader in no doubt that the poor man was guilty!

Mary Sandfod was an eighteen-year-old girl who lived about three miles from Ironbridge and had been going out on a regular basis with a twenty-two-year-old man, Samuel Johnson, who also came from the same area. Samuel was a married man but he still found the time to visit his young lady most evenings of the week.

On the evening of Wednesday 3 March 1822 Samuel had invited Mary to go to a dance with him to which she consented but when Samuel was walking towards the town he told her that he had a cold of sorts and did not feel well enough to go but would she go for a walk with him across the fields? Mary was heard to reply that she did not want to go for a walk and if Samuel would not go to the dance then she would go back home as she had a female friend coming to see her. Samuel managed to persuade her to go for a walk, and that was the last time Mary was seen alive.

Around 1 a.m. of Thursday 4 March, Samuel was seen walking on his own by a labourer friend, James Smith, who asked him where he had been so early in the morning. Samuel had replied that 'I have been no-where', and had hurried on. Later on that same morning the local farm owner, Mr Stubbs, was walking across his fields when he came across the signs of a struggle and immediately called the local constables, they combed the surrounding area and came across a shallow ditch in which the body of Mary was seen. Her mouth had been stuffed with hay, and a silk handkerchief had also been used to gag her. Her hands had been tied behind her back and there were numerous bruises on her head and body as well as puncture marks, also on her head and torso, inflicted by a pitchfork which was found close to Mary. It would appear that this was enough evidence for the jury and within just a few minutes the verdict was handed to the judge: 'guilty of murder'.

The judge then passed the normal sentence and instructed that Johnson be taken to the county gaol and hung. On the morning of Saturday 30 March 1822 Samuel Johnson was led out onto the roof of Shrewsbury Prison and without a word from him the executioner placed the hood over his head and pulled the lever which 'launched him into eternity'.

Samuels's body was taken down after the customary hour and his body sent to the Royal Salop Infirmary where it was to be used by the surgeons for dissection. Although Johnson never uttered a word at his hanging he did write a letter to his wife:

Dear Ellen,

If I may be allowed the expression I write to you for the purpose of expressing my thankfulness to you since my confinement, and I confess that I am deserving of my fate.

I would now fill up the last few remaining minutes of my existence in humble and earnest endeavours to deter any of you from coming to my sad end.

Had I resisted the first unlawful desire I should have crushed the seed from which sprang the hideous monster, Murder, had I listened to the advice of my parents I might have lived respectfully and died happy.

And now instead of my ashes mingling with the dust of my family and friends no grave is allowed for my resting place and no happy tongue shall 'Wish my spirit peace'.

I can say no more the bell calls me to an eternal world.

Believe me to be dear, Wife.

Your affectionate husband,
S.J.

Although the above is taken from *A full and particular account of the trial and execution of Samuel Johnson* by Mrs Wadeson, she omits to write anything in the handbill that could have been said in Samuel's defence, so did she think him guilty from the outset and so wrote this account from that angle? I think so. It can be seen that the final letter from Samuel to his wife was written from the heart and was a true account of his feelings, and not an ode as was the norm.

20

DEATH OF A SERGEANT

31 March 1828

Assize Judges:

Mr Justice Gaselee
Baron Vaughan

Grand Jury:

Lord Viscount Clive, Foreman.
T. W. W. Browne Esq.
Edward Cludde Esq.
William Charlton Esq.
Phillip Charlton Esq.
J. Whitehall Dod Esq.
Thomas Eyton Esq.
John Edwards Esq.
J.S. Edwardes Esq.
Thomas Harries Esq.
Francis K. Leighton Esq.
T. Whitmore MP
W. Whitmore Esq. MP
Sir E.J. Smythe Bart
P. Corbett Esq. MP
R. W. Smyth-Owen Esq.
John Wingfield Esq.
William Tayleur Esq.
T. Bulkeley-Owen Esq.
Robert Jenkins Esq.
Peter Broughton Esq.
Benjamin Flounders Esq.
T.C. Whitmore Esq.

William Stevenson, aged thirty-one, was a labourer who lived in Halesowen and on 3 April 1828 he was found guilty of the murder of John Horton in Oldbury. John Horton was a Sergeant at Law in the Oldbury Court and as such was a member of the barrister fraternity in the courts holding one of the highest ranks possible. He was also the keeper of Oldbury Gaol.

Stevenson was well known in the Oldbury criminal system as over the previous two years he had amassed no fewer than six cases of murder against him, all of which were carrying the death sentence. No one was keen to apprehend this particular felon as he had threatened to, 'Kill the first person to lay hands on him', nice chap to know! Such was his notoriety that although several attempts had been made to apprehend him no one would attempt his arrest on their own for fear of their own safety, although he had been told of the sentences hanging over him, all of which he chose to ignore. At some time Stevenson had managed to acquire an old sword that he had ground down to make a very evil-looking knife about 20in long and honed to a very sharp point and with this in his hands he had promised to, 'Cut the arms off any Oldbury man who came to take him'.

On the evening of 31 March 1828 around 7 p.m. Stevenson and a group of friends were drinking in the Whimsey public house in Oldbury when John Horton arrived after a tip off that he would find his man there. On spotting Stevenson, Horton approached him and proceeded to make his arrest. Stevenson asked for permission to return home to wash and change and Horton agreed, a decision that was to cost him his life. Stevenson went home and collected his knife and then returned to the pub and waved it in front of his friends, promising once again to kill any man who laid a hand on him. After a short while John Horton returned and on approaching Stevenson called for him to get up and follow him. Stevenson immediately sprang up and plunged the knife into Horton's body shouting, 'Now I am ready to go with you'. He then ran out of the pub still brandishing the knife in front of him and fleeing down the street. Horton made to follow him but collapsed on the door step and was taken upstairs to a room where, despite a desperate attempt to save his life by a local doctor, John Horton died six hours later, the knife having passed directly through the liver. He left a pregnant wife and five other children.

At the Shrewsbury Assizes held on 10 April the same year, a verdict of wilful murder was returned against William Stevenson and a large reward was offered for his capture.

In his summing up at the trial the judge questioned the conduct of Stevenson's friends as none of them made any attempt to take the knife from the man or warn Horton that he was armed and dangerous nor did any of them attempt to hold Stevenson after the attack.

It is not known how William Stevenson was captured but he was brought before the Shrewsbury Assizes held in the county hall in the square on Wednesday 29 July and after a very short trial lasting just a few minutes the judge passed the death sentence. *The Shrewsbury Chronicle* reporter wrote that at his trial:

The prisoner, although his eyes betokened considerable mental excitement, conducted himself calmly during his trial and when every other person in court shuddered at the atrocious details of the murder he remained unmoved. He had a peculiar cast of features, ferocious, with rather a turn to insanity, low forehead, projecting nose and high cheek bones.

When the judge asked Stevenson why the death sentence should not be passed, he broke into a tale of how he had been abused by the police constables, a tale which fell on many a deaf ear and made no mark on the judge as he let the death sentence stand. As Stevenson turned to leave the dock the gaol warder, Mr Whittaker, was seen to step forward and offer Stevenson a hand to which the condemned man pushed him away saying, 'Let me alone, I can go very well myself'.

On the day of his execution, Monday 4 August 1828, William Stevenson ascended the gallows stage with, 'A look of eager curiosity'. He even assisted the hangman with the placing of the noose and died, seemingly without any fuss or final words. After he had been left to hang for the prescribed hour, his body was cut down and sent to the Royal Salop Infirmary that stands behind St Mary's Church, for dissection.

21

SOME HANGMEN OF ENGLAND

It is probable that the executioner at William Stevenson's event was James Foxen who was hangman for England from 1820 until his death in 1829.

Foxen was replaced by William Calcraft who, despite most people's idea of a hangman, was a family man with two children and a pony that, so it is said, followed him around like a dog. Calcraft was England's hangman for forty-five years and his basic wages were around 25s a week with him receiving an extra guinea for each execution. If he had to travel outside of London then he commanded an extra £10 but if the felon was suddenly reprieved then Calcraft was paid just half of his fee. To supplement his income he also charged 2s 6d for each flogging he did as well as a charge for birching. Calcraft has his own niche in English penal history as being the man who officiated at the last public hanging of a woman, Frances Kidder, who was found guilty of murder and was hanged on 2 April 1868. He was also responsible for the last public execution of a man, Michael Barrett, who blew up the Clerkenwell House of Correction in order to rescue some of his colleagues. More than twelve people died in the ensuing blast at Clerkenwell with many more seriously injured although whether any of Barrett's friends were amongst the dead or injured is not known. It was Calcraft who led the man out onto the gallows on 26 May 1868.

On 13 August 1868 William Calcraft entered the history books again by being in charge of the first private execution that of Thomas Wells who was guilty of the murder of the station master at Dover. Wells was executed at Maidstone Gaol.

In 1874 it was decided that, at the ripe old age of seventy-five, it was time for William to hang up his noose which he did but under great protest passing away into the great gallows in the sky in 1879. William's place was taken by another William, William Marwood.

Up to this time the normal way of hanging someone was by the use of a short rope, sometimes just 2-3ft in length, and the death was more one of slow strangulation, sometimes death coming up to fifteen or twenty minutes later. Marwood was a man who was to change the way executions were conducted. By experimenting and calculations (how he experimented we are not quite sure), Marwood wrote to the authorities and suggested that by altering the length of the rope's fall to the weight and height of the criminal, it was possible to bring about an almost instantaneous death as the neck would be dislocated. The authorities agreed with Marwood and gave him the go-ahead. Marwood also invented a new type of noose; one with a metal ring through which the rope would slide more easily and this replaced

Early picture of William Marwood,
hangman from 1874.

the old hangman's knot. 'Weigh carefully and give as long a drop as possible' was Marwood's advice and although he only held the job for nine years, hangmen around the world soon followed his advice and thousands of felons should have been grateful to him for making their departure more easier.

As previously mentioned the hangmen who held sway on the scaffold before Marwood, John Langley, William Brunskill, Edward Dennis, James Botting and probably the most hated of all, Jack Ketch, all had one thing in common: they hanged by the book and were as callous as they came.

As well as devising the long drop and the new noose, Marwood also designed a new type of belt that went around the criminal's waist and had two other loops that held the arms fast against the side. This was to make sure that the condemned would not move too much and cause him more pain than was necessary.

This was exemplified when Marwood went to Armley Prison in Leeds to execute Charles Peace on 25 February 1879. As Marwood met Charles Peace in the condemned cell Peace asked, 'I do hope you will not punish me, I hope you will do your work quickly'.

Marwood eased his concerns by replying, 'You shall not suffer any pain from me'.

When felons went to the gallows and if hangmen were not careful, the criminals could get their hands between the rope and their neck in a vain attempt to stop the noose tightening. This would only give them more pain and once the rope had bit into the hands then they had to leave the poor guy to his awful fate. However, with Marwood's new belt design, it meant that their hands were secured and the hangman could do his job quickly and cleanly as Marwood did at Armley.

James Berry replaced Marwood in March 1884 and he devised a scale that took in the weight and height of the condemned and converted that to the required drop, even taking in the person's build and thickness of neck. But even with the scales things could still go wrong, and wrong they did go on 20 August 1891.

Berry had been booked to officiate at a hanging at Kirkdale Gaol in Liverpool and on arrival he had a bit of a ding-dong with Dr Barr, the prison doctor. Berry worked out that it would need a drop of 4ft 6in to remove the prisoner from this mortal coil but the good doctor believed that the drop should be 6ft 9in. After much arguing the doctor agreed to a length of 5ft 9in as long as Berry agreed which he did, but under protest, saying that if the head was pulled off then he would retire – prophetic words indeed because no sooner had the bolt been pulled and the body disappeared from view but the sound of dripping blood was heard. When officials entered the pit they found that the head had not been totally severed but the blood vessels in the neck had been ruptured, the head only being connected to the body by a few muscles!

22

A CASE OF MISTAKEN
IDENTITY?

20 August 1840

Judges:
Sir John Gurney
Sir John Taylor Coleridge

Grand Jury:
The Earl of Darlington MP, Foreman
Viscount Dungannon MP
Hon. H. W. Powys
Hon. Thomas Kenyon
Sir Baldwin Leighton Bart
Sir Edward J. Smythe Bart
Sir Rowland Hill Bart MP
Sir J. R. Kynaston Bart
Sir R. Jenkins, GCB MP
W. Ormsby Gore Esq. MP
T. C. Whitmore Esq. MP
W. Wolryche Whitmore Esq.
John Arthur Lloyd Esq.
Thomas Whitmore Esq.
John Wingfield Esq.
William Lloyd Esq.
C. Kynaston Mainwaring Esq.
William Sparling Esq.
Thomas Henry Hope Esq.
Thomas Eyton Esq.
Thomas Campbell Eyton Esq.

Any execution will bring out a crowd and at Tyburn the crowd could consist of hundreds of thousands of people but in more local sites they could only number in the hundreds.

Drawing of Josiah Mister as he stands in the dock at Shrewsbury to learn his fate.

When a crowd of 10,000 people descended on Shrewsbury on a fairly sunny day in 1841 the locals knew that they had a 'celebrity' in their midst.

Josiah Mister was a twenty-five-year-old who was known as a card sharp and pick-pocket but this young man drew this vast crowd to see his execution and it was not for pick-pocketing but for attempted murder.

Josiah had a history as a petty thief and as his father was unable to control him he had, as a last resort, sent him off to sea but after a short time Josiah returned to live with his brothers in Birmingham. One brother owned a hotel, the Crown Inn, and the other was in the brewing business but although they tried to keep him on the right side of the law he was soon in trouble.

After one episode with the Birmingham courts Josiah's brothers decided to give him some money to leave the country but he had other ideas on how to use this new-found wealth. In the early part of 1840 it was obvious that Josiah's money had run out as he was in trouble with the assizes in Hereford. He had been arrested on a charge of robbery and it was stated that he had stolen nearly £20 from a friend by hiding under this friend's bed and taking the money in the middle of the night. The outcome of that court hearing is unknown but after this Josiah began to run up unpaid debts across the Midlands.

He then turned his attentions on Shrewsbury and in the August of 1840 came to the Unicorn Hotel in the town to enquire about a certain gentleman named Mr Ludlow. Mr Ludlow was himself from Birmingham and followed the trade of cattle dealer but it is unknown whether the two men knew each other in the past. Be that as it may, somehow Josiah found out that Mr Ludlow would be travelling to the Shrewsbury Show and that afterwards he had a vast amount of money on him, almost £1,500. Josiah had asked a chambermaid at the Unicorn if Ludlow would be having a double room and the maid, rightly so as she saw that Josiah had no luggage with him, refused to tell him where he was staying. It turned out that Ludlow was sharing a double room with a gentleman, Mr Thomas Clarke from Welshpool, who normally stayed with relatives in Mardol. Once the Shrewsbury show had finished Josiah discovered that Mr Ludlow, still with his fortune, would be travelling to Ludlow, in south Shropshire, and began to make plans to relieve the traveller of some of his money. Josiah had been noted as constantly asking the agents in Ludlow when the Red Rover coach would be arriving from Shrewsbury and then walking a few miles out of Ludlow to Craven Arms, the last stop before Ludlow.

Once the Red Rover had arrived at the Angel Inn, Ludlow, Josiah appeared from the back of the coach and began the pretence that he had arrived with Mr Ludlow, even asking which room they would be sharing! Things now started to go wrong for Josiah so please enter our new member of the cast, Mr William Mackreth.

Mr Mackreth was a travelling salesman from Bristol and he had the misfortune to rent a room at the Angel on the night of 20 August, the room that was normally used by Mr Ludlow. Our salesman awoke some time in the early hours of the morning feeling a bit strange and when he put his hand to his throat he found that his hands were wet with blood – his.

The room being in darkness, William stumbled around for a while until he found the door and staggered out calling for help where he was found by one of the hotel staff.

It was discovered that William had had his throat slit by a razor, the cut being about 8in long stretching from ear to ear, and he had also received a puncture wound in the throat as well.

The *Eddowes Salopian Journal* wrote this description of the scene:

The scene of blood was the most frightful we ever witnessed, the object of the assassins knife presented a most appalling spectacle, room, passage, stairs were literally smeared and deluged in blood.

The landlord of the Angel, Mr Cooke, who was one of the first to discover him, thought at first that he had attempted to take his own life but this was not so. Mackreth was taken to a prominent surgeon in Ludlow, Mr Henry Hodges Esq. and gave his view on the attack to an escorting constable saying that he thought the attacker had hidden under his bed (where have we heard that before?). Mackreth had two razors in his possession but neither of them was used as the weapon.

A trail of blood led from Mackreth's room to room No. 20, Josiah's room, and he was the only person in the hotel that was found still in bed even with all the noise and kerfuffle going on around him.

On further investigation of Josiah's room blood was found on the curtains of the window overlooking a stable yard, the same yard that a blood-stained razor was found and there were traces of a substance called alum found in the basin of the room – alum is used to clean stains from clothing, and Josiah's shirt was wet and a lump of alum found in his shirt pocket. A towel was found to be missing from the room and Josiah had no idea where his stockings had gone!

After being questioned Josiah was seen skulking down the back stairs with a package under his coat. The package was a towel and a pair of stockings and he was later seen in the stable yard looking around for something, a razor maybe?

All of the above information was reported in the *Eddowes Journal* and other newspapers and it could be said that this was one court case where the final outcome was decided upon by the press:

> Even Mackreth himself pleaded to the judge for leniency saying: 'I am convinced without a shadow of a doubt that Josiah Mister alone was the man who made the attack upon my life in Ludlow'.
>
> In April of 1841 Mackreth again put pen to paper expressing: 'My astonishment that an innocent man had been sacrificed' and, 'Not once had Mister provided any positive explanations against him'.

Public interest in the case was great and scores of people waited outside the court in hope of seeing anyone connected with the case, or Josiah himself. In fact so great was this interest that it is reported that forty-seven of the local magistrates arrived in the hope of being retained for service on the grand jury.

As we can see William Mackreth survived the attack although he was scarred for life. Local sympathy was directed at Josiah – whoever heard of anyone being condemned to hanging for an attempted murder when even the victim of the attack petitioned for clemency?

Despite petitions from all sides and people pointing out the youthfulness of Josiah the judge, Baron Gurney passed the sentence of death and Josiah was led away.

The day of Josiah Mister's execution was described by the *Eddowes Journal*: 'The day was beautiful, the sun was shining as the visible eye of heaven upon all around but for this unhappy man there would be no more earth, no more sunshine'.

The Shrewsbury Chronicle reported the execution thus:

> He wore the same attire he had on during the trial, we thought him very little altered in appearance since his trial. His complexion, which was then a clear olive, had grown very sallow and the muscles under his eyes were swollen – we presume from weeping, as he had a handkerchief in his hand, which he applied to his eyes at intervals. His hair, which he combed very much on one side, had struggled out of place and nearly covered his left eye. His countenance had a very sad expression it was comparatively calm but it was the calmness of despair.

The reporters on these newspapers, as has been mentioned before, had to paint a picture in words so that those reading them could almost see for themselves what had taken place. I leave it to the unknown reporter of *The Shrewsbury Chronicle* to describe Josiah Mister's last moments on this earth, a victim of mistaken identity gone tragically wrong:

> Mister appeared in tears on the drop, He knelt and prayed and the multitude were hushed with awe, even the most careless felt that a soul was returning to him who had sent it forth

in a frail vessel of mortality. The executioner adjusted the rope and Mister took a last look around him before grasping the hand of Mr Hopewell, the turnkey who had charge of him, saying 'Good-bye, may God bless you, I freely forgive the jury'. The executioner pulled back the bolt, the drop fell with a loud crash and Mister was launched into eternity. He struggled violently for about two minutes, the first convulsive motion of the muscles bring the hands nearly together in front, the next carried them a little backwards, the third brought them up in the air as far as the pinioning would allow and the last left them firmly clenched by his side. The culprits stomach heaved strongly three or four times as if the trunk were about separating from the extremities.

Another journalist wrote: 'The inexpressible horror excited by the prisoner's appearance became instantly visible and the crowds of persons hurried from the dreadful scene in all directions, those who remained witnessed struggles and convulsions distressing to behold for two minutes'.

It was the common practice for the hangman, the officials and all others to depart the scaffold as soon as the bolt was drawn, just leaving the body for the compulsory hour but the crowd that departed rapidly could place a certain amount of blame on the heavens for:

The crowd dispersed rapidly being urged in their retreat by the threatening aspect suddenly assumed by the weather. At half past twelve very few people were left, and then came on a brief storm of wind and rain and the gibbet and it's victim were alone'

The executioner for Josiah Mister, dressed in his smock-frocked coat and oilskin hat, was from Stourbridge and he received the usual fee of 10 guineas plus 10s 6d for travelling expenses. When asked if he was going to sell Josiah's clothes, as was the norm, he replied, 'Oh dear no, I always wears them!' but a spectator did manage to acquire Josiah's handkerchief for 1s.

23

THE END IS NIGH!

After the abolition of public hangings, executions still carried on but behind the closed doors of the prisons.

In Shrewsbury the first private hanging was of William Samuels who was hanged on 28 July 1886 and was conducted by James Berry. Samuels committed a murder in Welshpool of a Mr William Marrott by giving him strychnine and although the crime had been in Montgomery and it was up to the high sheriff of that county, Mr P.A. Beck Esq. and his under-sheriff, Mr G.D. Harrison to arrange the execution, it was agreed that the deed would be done in Shrewsbury.

Timbers from the old scaffold were used and this was erected close to the site of the old prison infirmary and a pit, 4ft sq. and 10ft 6in deep was dug with the platform level with the ground. This meant that when the bolt was drawn the condemned man literally fell from view and all that the public would know the execution having taken place was the flying of a black flag from the pole above the main door.

With the execution planned for 8 a.m. on the Monday James Berry would arrive in Shrewsbury either on the Saturday or Sunday and would lodge in the prison itself. Earlier in the week a parcel arrived at the prison, 'Causing great consternation amongst the public of the town', as it was reported in *The Shrewsbury Chronicle*. It was thought that the parcel contained the rope for the execution but James always provided his own.

Mr Berry was a dour, bearded and moustached Yorkshireman who lived in Bradford, a shoemaker by trade and was chosen from over 2,000 applicants. Mr Berry's fees for executions were £10 a head (no pun intended!) plus his travel expenses and if the condemned were reprieved then he received half his fee. During his term of office in 1883, James officiated at 117 hangings, but not all in Shrewsbury.

The last execution to take place in Shrewsbury occurred in 1960 when a young man, George Riley, was executed for the murder of a middle-aged widow. Many people believed, and still believe, that George was innocent and the prisoners in Shrewsbury jail showed their support for George as he was led to the gallows by banging their cups on the walls of their cells and lighting fires. The drawing of that bolt in 1960 also draws to a close the history of executions in Shrewsbury.

Other local titles published by The History Press

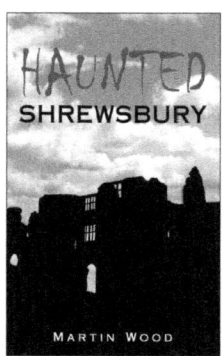

Haunted Shrewsbury
MARTIN WOOD

From accounts of poltergeists to first-hand encounters with ghouls, this collection of tales compiled by Shrewsbury's illustrious town crier contains a chilling range of ghostly goings-on. Discover the restless apparition at the castle gates, ghostly monks from the abbey church and a whole family of spirits in Milk Street. This phenomenal gathering of spooks in Shrewsbury will captivate anyone interested in the supernatural history of the area.

978 0 7524 4303 4

Around Shrewsbury Volume II
DEREK M. WALLEY

This book examines the different aspects of life in a mainly agricultural community and shows the numerous changes in local streets, schools, churches and factories that were produced by social and economic progress, which was often both spectacular and memorable. This collection of old photographs and postcards will bring back memories of history of Shrewsbury and is a good companion volume to *Around Shrewsbury.*

978 0 7524 3371 4

Breweries and Bottlers of Wellington
ALLAN FROST

With a full account from medieval times until brewing and bottling ceased in 1969, this book explores the business successes and failures of The Shropshire, The Mill Field, The Red Lion, The Union, The Botanical and The Wrekin Brewery. Lavishly illustrated with plans, memorabilia and many previously unpublished photographs, this is the definitive history of brewing and bottling in the historic medieval market town of Wellington in Shropshire.

978 0 7524 4631 8

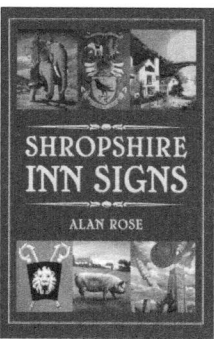

Shropshire Inn Signs
ALAN ROSE

This book takes the reader on a tour of Shropshire's inns past and present, discovering the origins of names such as The Kangaroo, The Eagle and Serpent and The Blue Boar. Illustrated with over 100 images, *Shropshire Inn Signs* lists the huge variety found around the county and offers a fascinating insight into the history of these highly crafted items. It will delight all those interested in the story behind the signs, as well as proving to be a valuable guide for those who wish to locate them.

978 0 7524 3843 6

If you are interested in purchasing other books published by The History Press, or in case you have difficulty finding any History Press books in your local bookshop, you can also place orders directly through our website
www.thehistorypress.co.uk